Writing History!

Jeannette Kamp
Susan Legêne
Matthias van Rossum
Sebas Rümke

Writing

History!

A COMPANION FOR HISTORIANS

AMSTERDAM UNIVERSITY PRESS

Originally published as *Geschiedenis schrijven! Wegwijzer voor historici* by Jeannette Kamp, Susan Legêne, Matthias van Rossum and Sebas Rümke (2016).
© Amsterdam University Press

Translation: Jill Bradley Language Services

Cover and interior design: V3-Services v.o.f., Baarn

ISBN   978 94 6298 639 8
e-ISBN   978 90 4853 762 4 (pdf)
DOI   10.5117/9789462986398
NUR   680

© Jeannette Kamp, Susan Legêne, Matthias van Rossum & Sebas Rümke / Amsterdam University Press B.V., Amsterdam 2018

Contents

INTRODUCTION

Historians do not only know a lot about the past, what we conventionally call history, by writing about it they also *make* history. By interacting with other historians, both past and present, and in dialogue with the public of their own time they contribute knowledge and insights that help a society to be conscious of its relation to the past. This does not only apply to the history of our most recent times: thinking about history is interesting and relevant from the earliest appearance of the humans as distinctive creatures on this planet. History is about a past that can be constantly approached from countless angles with new ideas, insights and techniques – and that is why there is an exclamation mark in the title of this guide. *Writing History!* appeals to the ambition to actively explore the possibilities of the discipline and then encourages you to follow your own path.

An important key to writing history is the historical method of source criticism, which is also a recurring subject in this companion. Most historical methods and techniques have been developed through what we would call an 'analogue' context: starting from unique archival documents, printed books, collections of objects, visual sources and recorded accounts and stories. However, the rapid developments in information and communication technology as well as digital imaging techniques do have a great deal of influence on the methods and techniques of writing history. They change the access to our sources as the sources themselves acquire a different character. Communication between historians about their results is taking on new forms and archiving is done in new ways. Prospective historians are in the middle of these changes and will help to determine their impact on the historian's craft.

This companion is therefore a 2.0 version – it does not anticipate technological innovations and what the future might hold with respect to using 'big data', image recognition, the reconstruction of historical sounds and other developments we can expect. *Writing History!* is intended to connect the customary academic historical methods and techniques and the digital means that are now available to the historian. IT puts source criticism in a new light. It is also important as it expands the historical debate, both by reducing geographical divisions and by offering more opportunities for immediate interaction with readers. A conscious use of methods and techniques for our discipline will allow prospective historians to make an important contribution to such renewal.

The Dutch edition of *Writing History!* is about practising history in the Dutch language, which, of course, is not the same as practising Dutch history. Likewise, the English version of this book is not about writing a history of the English-speaking world, but about practicing history in English. However, language is not just a neutral vehicle for communication; different language traditions have generated differences in historiography as well. *Writing History!* does not explore such differences, but offers a translation of the Dutch companion, in order to facilitate its use as a course book in both Dutch/English bilingual and in English history programmes. The book is structured as a guide to historical methods and techniques. It is aimed at everyone who wants to develop the skills needed for writing history, both within and outside of academia. We hope that all prospective historians find this book to be a useful companion as they write history.

STRUCTURE OF THE BOOK

Writing History! consists of six chapters and concludes with two technical appendices.

Chapter 1 discusses the process of historical research in general, the emphasis being on the importance of formulating a good historical research question. All the phases and techniques of historical research are dealt with briefly and will be addressed in more detail in the following chapters.

1.1 Subject and research question: designating a subject / types of question: descriptive, explanatory, exploratory / the research question/ criteria for historical research questions

1.2 Orientation and questions: the historical context: *status quaestionis* / availability of sources / your own contribution to writing history

1.3 Standpoint and historical debate: criticism and self-criticism/ defining your position: facts, interpretations and philosophical viewpoints

1.4 The research plan: questions, material and methods, planning: main question, sub-questions, structure / planning and feedback

In Chapter 2, the emphasis is on the building blocks of historical research: literature and sources. It deals with the distinction between primary sources and secondary literature, the diversity of primary sources and how these are embedded in various academic disciplines and traditions of collecting, with a brief indication of how you can find them in libraries, archives and museums.

2.1 Primary and secondary sources: primary sources: originating from the context / secondary sources: academic historical literature

Chapter 3, which deals with how to apply the historical method, discusses how you do research with the help of a step-by-step plan. When searching for and organising information, you must constantly make intrinsic choices – where to look and how to read, how to collect your sources and how to interpret them. All these actions require you to make conscious decisions and to repeatedly return to your research question. Next, we deal with a number of methodological questions about using literature and researching your sources.

Chapter 4 continues with a focus on the writing process. Writing is a concentrated way of thinking that compels you to formulate a train of thought clearly. However, it is also a technique and of great importance to a convincing historical presentation. Moreover, for historical accounts there are a number of conventions concerning notes with which every historian should be thoroughly acquainted. In discussing the structure of a text – its overall structure and on the level of paragraphs and sentences – we shall address the intrinsic aspects of the voice of the author and the implicit or explicit debate of which they are a part.

Chapter 5 addresses the 'oral' variant. Speaking and writing are related
to each other, but still fundamentally different. This chapter deals with
various forms and styles of giving a presentation and the importance of
you, yourself, taking part in the historical debate. Oral presentation and
debate are just as important for preparing for a career as a historian in the
history course as being able to report in writing.

Chapter 6 very briefly considers the practice of the discipline. Historians' relationship, written and oral, to their colleagues and to society as
a whole, is based on their study and knowledge of the past. In this, depending on the subject, opinions about the present can play a role. Historians are not oracles who can clarify the present or foretell the future.
Generally speaking, they are somewhat reticent about giving their 'historical judgement'; interpretation, offering a context – that is primarily
the field in which historians are trained. This guide intends to contribute
to that training in the hope of offering a good basis for the future practice as a historian.

The guide concludes with two appendices. Appendix I consists of the
guidelines according to 'De Buck' that are most commonly used for notes
in historical research in Dutch-language publications. They have been
put in a separate appendix to facilitate consultation. Publications in other
countries or related (social sciences) disciplines use too many different
styles of annotation to be dealt with here.
Appendix II contains a brief presentation of a number of those other styles
of annotation.

1 HISTORICAL RESEARCH: THE IMPORTANCE OF THE RESEARCH QUESTION

1.1 **Subject and question:** designating a subject / types of question: descriptive, explanatory, exploratory / the research question / criteria for historical research questions

1.2 **Orientation and questions: The historical context:** *status quaestionis* / the savailability of sources / your own contribution to writing history

1.3 **Standpoint and historical debate:** criticism and self-criticism / defining your position: facts, interpretations, and philosophical viewpoints

1.4 **The research plan: Questions, material and methods, planning:** main question, sub-questions, structure / planning and feedback

Historians provide insight into the past. By means of books, articles, websites, or presentations, they offer information to colleagues, students, and a wider public. In their work, historians constantly ask questions about the past, and they answer those questions by researching historical literature and sources. But how do you design a justified academic historical research project? How do you find a relevant subject, and how do you then define it? How do you formulate a good research question? Once you have your question, what are the next steps? This chapter deals with what you should take into account when setting up a research project. It addresses how a subject should be chosen, how to formulate a research question, and how to define your research in relation to the literature and source material. It also discusses how to go about organising the research, the role of advisers/supervisors, and how to handle comments and advice.

1.1 Subject and research question

Academic research is driven by various motives. It could be admiration for something beautiful or exceptional, interest in the working of certain processes, or concern about current questions. Sometimes a research question is born of the urge to show that something that is regarded as true is not so, or that it is not so simple or one-sided as it is represented by others. Curiosity, admiration, and even indignation – these are all legitimate motives. Your circumstances also influence what you find interesting, so it is important to reflect explicitly on how you arrive at a subject.

1.1.1 Designating a subject

When following a history programme, you might simply be given the task of writing about a certain subject. Historians also carry out research commissioned by third parties in the context of a broader research pro- *commission* gramme into which they bring their more specific interests and expertise. However, it is certainly all right to choose your research subject out of a purely personal interest if there is the opportunity to do so, for example *interest* when you write your Bachelor's or Master's thesis. In such cases, your topic could be simply a subject that appeals to you, suits your future plans, or requires certain talents that you want to develop. At the same time, when choosing a subject, you must bear in mind what contribution your research can make to the discipline or to society at large.

It is important to be aware of all these considerations. Critical examination of your choice of subject – even if your subject is not of your own free choice – is the first crucial step to realising your research. It can be useful to ask yourself questions that challenge the obviousness of your choice. Why is this particular subject so interesting? What would you like to know? What results do you expect that researching that subject will produce?

As a rule, historical research concerns both the discipline and the larger society, and therefore both academic and social values can come into play when judging a particular piece of research or the choice of subject. Establishing a well-defined balance between these values is practically impossible. Despite the various efforts of governments and universities to make academic results measurable ('valorisation', 'social relevance'), determining the relevance of a specific research subject and the importance of its results remains a subjective matter.

academic and social value

Since a fixed relationship between *academic* and *social* relevance does not exist, the balance between the two must be sought with each new subject. In general, we can say that academic research aims at pushing and developing our knowledge and insight in the broadest sense. The social effect of this knowledge – for instance, how it contributes to the solution of societal problems – is of major importance. Such a contribution can come from individual research or can be the result of the insights of a specific discipline and also concerns the spread of scientific knowledge and fundamental attitudes in general. However, the academic relevance of every research project is a primary condition in the first place. The primary way in which an academic work will be judged is how it contributes to the discipline and to the academic process of knowledge production. This process consists of both building up new knowledge and insights and examining, criticising, and sometimes demolishing existing knowledge and insights that are no longer satisfactory.

knowledge

knowledge production

The choice of a particular subject and the set-up of the research are somewhere on this spectrum between new data to be explored or new knowledge to be developed, and the re-evaluation of existing knowledge. Determining a subject is a strategic action in which these factors must be borne in mind.

strategic act

1.1.2 Types of question: Descriptive, explanatory, exploratory

How does the choice of a good subject lead to the next step – a good research project? Designing a sound historical research project begins with the formulation of a question. Phrasing the question implies that you formulate as precisely as possible what you want to find out by conducting this research. Even more than in the choice of subject, the value of the research lies in the problem definition. To put it simply, a good research question is half the work.

formulating a question

There are questions of all types. Some questions are 'big' and deal, for instance, with a long-term historical development or a problem of global format. However, questions can also be 'smaller' and concern a specific historical event, a specific theme, or a short period. The big questions are usually divided into smaller sub-questions. The answer to a small question might be crucial to find new approaches to a bigger question. By subdividing bigger research questions into separate questions, they become more manageable. The choice of such sub-questions is not arbitrary: addressing them produces a systematic and incremental answer to the main research question.

sub-questions

A research question, then, is very different from the 'search term' that you almost certainly type into a search engine several times a day; nor is it a 'frequently asked question' to which a pre-formulated answer will appear that briefly outlines what is or what should be done. A good historical research question does not just seek an answer to important questions of 'who, what, where, when, how, and why' but also tries to find a greater depth of insight into a particular problem. When formulating the question, its quality and feasibility are of crucial importance. Moreover, it is important to look at the chosen research question in relation to other, often bigger problems. Does the answer to the question of your research lead to new insights or new questions with a broader scope?

In general, we distinguish the following types of questions – descriptive, explanatory, and exploratory questions. *Descriptive questions* ask about aspects and characteristics of a subject. The question often leads to a description that does not make any judgment on the subject of the text. Frequently, the knowledge gained from a descriptive question is necessary to reach an explanatory question. *Explanatory questions* seek the reasons for a particular phenomenon or other connections between phenomena. The question directs a search for an explanation of a phenomenon or process. Lastly, *exploratory questions* can be assessing, prescriptive, or advisory. An exploratory question, having the nature of an assessment, attempts to examine or test an existing expectation or explanation. This can be done by very 'directly' testing a theory or hypothesis on a case that until that point had not been researched. It can also test 'indirectly' by making a comparison between various situations or phenomena or by comparing a specific phenomenon with a standard or reference point.

descriptive questions

explanatory questions

exploratory questions

Exploratory questions have a *prescriptive* or *advisory* character, for instance when the research tests concepts or methods and formulates conclusions on their use. Policy research can be exploratory as well. Historians are well equipped for this type of research, but they must bear in mind the tensions that can arise between the various interests involved in academic research and the social adaptation of that research. A good, academically sound exploratory question must always meet certain academic standards, and the insights acquired by descriptive and explanatory research questions will often be necessary for this.

1.1.3 The research question

examples A closer look at the research questions posed by others in an academic study might help to understand what a research question is. There are countless examples, of course, because almost every academic text is structured around a historically relevant research question that is to be found in the text, either explicitly or implicitly. The research question presents the aim immediately as well as the direction and often the delineation of the research that lies behind a particular text.

To give an example: in her study *De draad in eigen handen [Taking it in your own hands]* about women in the early modern Dutch textile industry, Elise van Nederveen Meerkerk states her main question as 'How can the division of labour between men and women be explained, and which factors caused possible changes in the pre-industrial period?'[1] This is an *explanatory* question because it seeks an explanation for – that is, the causes of – the division of labour between men and women and possible changes in that division. However, note that with this question an explanation is sought for something that must first be described. So the descriptive question underlying this research reads: 'How was work divided up between men and women in the textile industry and what changes possibly occurred during the early modern period?'[2] In this case, the historian examined the historical subject using literature and her own primary source research at a *descriptive* level in order to then research her main *explanatory* question.

Sometimes, it is more difficult to differentiate between *descriptive* and *explanatory* questions. In a study of unmarried mothers in the countryside in the southern Netherlands, Sofie De Langhe, Maja Mechant, and Isabelle Devos ask the question: 'In what way did the socio-economic context of an area influence the various aspects of the lives of unmarried mothers?'[3]

At first sight, this question appears to have an explanatory nature because it points to an interpretation of the connection between social and economic environmental factors and the lives of unmarried mothers. Nevertheless, the research question is primarily *descriptive* because the words 'in what way' in fact indicate a description of the influence of the environmental factors on the lives of unmarried mothers. From this description, the historians must then find the *explanation* of the specific causes and effects they want to demonstrate.

1.1.4   Criteria for historical research questions

It is therefore possible to ask all kinds of questions in all sorts of ways. Nevertheless, not every potential question is a good question. A number of criteria are important to come to a sound historical research question. First, a question must always be formulated as precisely as possible; a question should not be obscure, should not contain generalities or ambiguities and, lastly, it must meet a number of academic criteria. Vagueness in the question can lead to the research diverging from the point. It is also possible that the researcher with an unclear question believes that the aim of the research is clear, though in fact that is not the case. Novice researchers often fall into this trap. There is nothing wrong with making some adaptations to the research question during the process of research, but it is a great hindrance if the weakness of a research question is determined late in the research process, as this could lead to loss of time or to the failure of the research.

justified historical research questions

The character or types of question must be clear from how they are worded. Interrogatory words such as 'how', 'whereby', and 'why' are good indicators of the nature of a question. When a question is formulated as a well-phrased sentence, it is important that the verbs used give a clear indication of the type of research question. Emphatically presenting the main question of the research in the text can help the historian to write a well-flowing argument and also keep the readers' attention on the problem.

Moreover, a good question must satisfy a number of academic criteria. A question must be one that is historically relevant. Questions that approach a subject in a technical, psychological, medical, or geographical manner cannot always be answered by historical research. The question must also open up various options for examination in greater depth. For instance, it is not really useful to ask a question that can only be answered with a name, a concept, a summary or a simple 'yes', 'no', or 'just a bit'. Some may try to avoid this by beginning a question with 'to what extent...', but it is advisable to be cautious in applying this solution: a 'to what extent...' question has the tendency to cloak a weak question.

academic criteria

An academic research question should not contain any implicit value judgment. If you choose to take a normative approach, you should say so explicitly. A question must be concrete and state clearly what is being researched. It must also be realistic – executable in terms of the time and sources available for research.

1.2 Orientation and questions: The historiographical context

So far, we have looked at what sorts of questions can be asked and what criteria a good research question must satisfy. But how do you formulate a question? How can you compose a good and relevant research question? Like the choice of an interesting subject, questions do not simply come to mind. They start with an orientation phase. Defining a good question is based on: 1) a thorough knowledge of the relevant academic literature, 2) a preliminary exploration of the available (source) material, and 3) an assessment of its potential contribution to the discipline. The purpose of the research – the matter you want your question to answer – must be related to these three elements. The better idea you have of the context, the more precise your research question will be.

1.2.1 *Status quaestionis*

status quaestionis

With the help of a provisional research question, you can chart the existing knowledge on the subject by exploring the literature. It is important to know what has already been researched and from which various perspectives the subject has been studied. A good way to reach this insight is to make a systematic analysis of the findings already published – a *status quaestionis* (Latin for state of the research). Historians call the *status quaestionis* a historiographical overview, that is, a critical and analytical overview of the developments in historical writing on the subject. Such a discussion of existing knowledge in academic literature shows what is known and what still needs to be explored. The *status quaestionis* also makes clear from which approaches the various relevant texts have been written and what debates the relevant authors have held about the research subject. The *status quaestionis* links the knowledge or assertions found in the literature with the research on which it is based. It thus shows how various sorts of sources and research methods can lead to different viewpoints. Moreover, in this way it provides a brief impression of which sources are used for what, and what they are not suitable for. A *status quaestionis* does not need to be limited to a discussion of academic historical works: depending on the research question, references to memoirs, political writings, policy documents, cultural products, or results found in other academic disciplines can be relevant in describing the state of research concerning a specific subject.

The main purpose of a *status quaestionis* is to chart the academic historical debate and sometimes the social debate too. Sometimes, these debates are easily recognisable because authors explicitly argue about a difference in insight. At other times, the differences in insight remain implicit; the authors do not refer to each other, and their work only touches on that of the others by means of their new research question. In such cases, it is even more important to make your own comparison between the various viewpoints found in the literature. By approaching the literature in this systematic fashion, you can sometimes obtain surprising new insights into important themes, controversies, or questions that have not yet been sufficiently researched and can give shape and urgency to your own research question (see also Chapter 4). *recognising debates*

___

1.2.2 The availability of sources

It is also important to obtain an overview of the source material available for your research. By sources, we mean every sort of documentation that directly originates from the period that the historian is researching. Historical research can take place on the basis of many sorts of sources, which can vary from written texts to buildings, from photographs to objects, and from interviews to sermons (see also Chapter 3). It is essential that the selected source material is really suitable for the research question. The question has to be answered on the basis of the source material selected. Obtaining a solid overview of the available sources and the advantages and disadvantages of the various materials is a crucial building block for the formulation of your definitive research question. Bear in mind not only the availability of the sources but also issues such as their reliability, legibility, the nature of information they contain, and their size and quantity. *obtaining an overview of available sources*

___

1.2.3 Your own contribution to writing history

The exploration of literature and sources on the basis of a provisional research question is necessary to be able to formulate very precisely how the answering of that question will contribute to the sum of knowledge in the discipline of history. It frequently happens that, due to this exploratory phase, the research question must be adapted or formulated anew. On the basis of insight into the existing literature, you can determine what is already known, the perspectives that have been taken on the subject, and which perspectives are dominant. This knowledge is important for the formulation (or reformulation) of the research question because the research question indicates what can, or must, be added to the academic discipline to which the research belongs. The proposed research initiated by the research question always relates to the results and statements *(re)formulating the research question* of earlier academic work. This is also the case with subjects that so far have remained unstudied or insufficiently studied. The lack of research into a certain subject could be caused by a dominant historical view that assumes that the existing insights into the subject are sufficient or that considers a theme as completely irrelevant or does not recognise or acknowledge sources as sources.

Viewed this way, setting up a research project on the basis of a specific research question is in itself a historiographical activity. It is the *contribution to* preparation for making a contribution to the writing of history. While *writing history* setting up your research project, consider how your research question is related to earlier studies. This seems evident with subjects that have been the object of much research but it is also true of subjects of which little is known. In both cases, reflect upon the contribution that the new research will hopefully make in regard to earlier studies of the same historical subject. Consider, too, what kind of impact the possible results of the new research might have on the broader historiographical context.

With subjects that have been historically researched extensively, it is often easier to formulate an *explanatory* or *exploratory* research question. It is then possible to focus, either implicitly or explicitly, on the insights and explanations of earlier studies when developing your own research question. With subjects for which little historical research has been carried out, this can be more difficult, particularly – even in studies with a more overarching character – if there are few or no statements in which relations of cause and effect are assumed or suggested. In that case, a more *descriptive* research question is the more obvious choice. With such a *descriptive* research question, it is particularly important to indicate the possible implications of the newly acquired insights for the understanding of broader themes or developments. After all, no subject stands alone. Research always falls within a broader framework or narrative (see Chapter 4) – however big, small, specific, or thematic a subject is.

1.3   Standpoint and historical debate

link The research question can be regarded as the link between the proposed research, the state of historical knowledge (the literature on a specific subject and larger historical themes), and the available research *lever* material: or, if you want to start a discussion, regard it as a lever. A strategically chosen research question can lead to new insights that make an important contribution to a debate or can break open an existing consensus. With such a debate, it can be useful to highlight the verifiable or falsifiable statements or the assertions from the literature on your subject and position your research in relation to them. Make sure that you do not simplify these earlier statements: do not make the work of other historians into a 'straw man' that you burn in your research.

In the social sciences, it is usual to use the conclusions of earlier studies to formulate a *hypothesis* that can be examined in the proposed research. This is also sometimes possible with historical research. A *hypothesis* is a provisional assumption that must be examined for its validity. Often a hypothesis contains statements of expectations concerning a particular phenomenon. Therefore, the hypothesis does not necessarily need to be based on the same historical subject that is the main focus of the new research. The results of studies of comparable cases – bearing in mind possible similarities and differences – can form the basis for your own hypothesis as well. Link or lever – in the end, a good research question must ensure that the research project makes a relevant contribution to the state of knowledge in an academic field. When given the answer to a trivial research question, the reader's reaction might be to shrug and say 'So what?'

hypothesis

1.3.1   Criticism and self-criticism

Research does not happen in a vacuum. Academics constantly discuss their research questions and plans with each other so that their criticism and advice can lead to adjustments and improvements. In history programmes, discussions in class not only offer practice in formulating research questions, they also involve the participants in the social and collegial process of giving constructive academic criticism. Such constructive criticism is essential for assessing the viability of plans and ideas. In the early phase of research, such critical exchange helps to reveal imperfections in the research question and the research set-up (see also Chapter 5).

constructive academic criticism

Moreover, writing history requires the capability of critical reflection on your own research process. Reread your research question regularly and ask yourself whether it really defines your intention in a comprehensible way. Is there any vagueness and does it have historical merit? Is the question well-defined? Is the subject not too big or the expected answer too trivial? To get to the heart of it, ask yourself 'So what?' about the relevance of the research or its results. The answer will help to define in more detail why it is important that this research is carried out, what new insights the research will produce, and their relevance. These are questions you can ask about your own research before approaching anyone else. Asking such questions leads to self-reflection and to mak-

'so what?'

(self-)reflection

ing your research plan more precise. In fact, it is the touchstone of the research structure as the research question connects the existing knowledge, the material available, and the new proposed research in a useful manner.

1.3.2 Defining your position: Facts, interpretations, and philosophical viewpoints

defining one's own position
When setting up a research question and plan, it is advisable to consider your own position. Do you want your research to yield an explanation of a historical phenomenon or development? Do you want to test whether the accepted opinions are really valid? Or do you want to look at a phenomenon from a different viewpoint? Particularly in the case of those subjects about which decided opinions dominate the academic debate, it is important to be conscious of your own position and role. Do not worry about taking a stance, but remember that you must always have good arguments for your position. The conscious refusal to take a clear position in an academic debate also requires a solid argument.

'good' historical explanation
Generations of philosophers of history have wrestled with the question of what is a 'good' historical explanation. Over the course of time, a great variety of answers have been proposed. Some historians are of the opinion that a historical explanation is only scientific when it is based *empirical regularities* on empirical regularities (the 'positivists'). Others claim that a historical explanation must grasp the meaning that lies behind actions and events and make these comprehensible (the 'hermeneutics'). There is also the *construction* argument that the narrative is self-explanatory and, as the historian's construction, has its own independence or autonomy in respect to the past (the 'narrativists'). In this view, the validity of a historical explanation depends on such factors as scope, originality, and persuasiveness. These are questions for the philosophy of history that will not be further discussed in this companion, but they do relate, either explicitly or implicitly, to every historical research project.

This is also true of the changes that are the result of information and communication technology (ICT) that have provided a different way of accessing historical data and allowed new narrative and visual forms to *Digital History* present research outcomes. Some refer to this development as 'Digital History'; others, taking their cue from 'e-Science', prefer to call it 'e-History', whereby the 'e' stands not only for *electronic* but also for *enhanced* – that is, improved, extended. This ICT development gives a new turn to the discussion about digital hermeneutics – to the interpretation of the data and phenomena that the computer makes digitally visible and the patterns related to the past that the technique generates.

Accurately reproducing the facts is not sufficient for a good historical account. A historian without a research question who just gives a summary of unrelated historical facts cannot be accused of falsehood but does leave the reader simply confounded. A simple summary of facts that are directly related contributes little to historical knowledge. For example, look at the following summary of facts about the French Revolution: 'The storming of the Bastille took place in 1789, Louis XIV was decapitated. Napoleon Bonaparte came to power in 1799.' This form of histori- *chronicle* cal writing is a *chronicle* – a chronological summary of related historical facts. The academically trained historian does not just communicate to the reader what has happened in the past but why this happened and what the (historical) significance of it is. To do this, the historian must select, interpret, and explain. Debates about history, to which you must *selection,* pay attention in a *status quaestionis*, do not deal only with the question of *interpretation, and* whether certain historical happenings are presented accurately but pri- *explanation* marily with how such incidents must be interpreted and explained. In this, the historiographical tradition in which the historian works plays an important role.

Writing a historical text bears some relation to literary writing. Chap- *literary writing* ter 4 discusses the more technical aspects of writing. Like the novelist, the historian integrates events and occurrences in a narrative structure that turns them into a cohesive whole. This is an important reason why some argue strongly that history must be considered a discipline of the humanities and not a social science – which does not alter the fact that there are overlaps between these disciplines, for example because historians may make use of social science methods. However, there is an essential difference between a historical and a literary text. The historian's text has claims to validity that must be substantiated, while the text of a *claims of validity* literary writer is free from such constraints.

1.4 The research plan: Questions, material and methods, planning

Let us return to the craft of writing history. Setting up a research project means more than choosing a subject, formulating a good research question, and thinking about the nature of your sources that will give you the necessary facts to examine relations. In this early stage of your research, you should also think about 'operationalising' your research. A *operationalising* research plan is needed for this – a step-by-step plan for carrying out the research.

1.4.1 Main question, sub-questions, structure

sub-questions

Firstly, the research question is split into various sub-questions. Together, these sub-questions form an elaboration of the main question. Answering the separate sub-questions should lead to the *systematic* and *incremental* answer to the main question.

research plan

In addition to the main and sub-questions, the research plan provides an overview of the structure of your argument – the chapters you have planned, the hypothesis, the sources and literature. The plan also gives information about the approach you have planned and a *status quaestionis* could also be added. The information about the approach is not just a summary of the available sources, it is first and foremost the method that will be used for approaching these sources. Which techniques will be necessary, for instance? (Think of palaeography for manuscripts, interview techniques for oral history, statistics for numerical material, text mining for searching through large digitalised text collections, knowledge of the material for tangible objects as historical sources, etc.) Explain clearly what sources you will examine and when and why. For example, it might be necessary to set the research up using samples, say sample years, or to execute suitable sample years to take a broader sample. In that case, it is necessary to give your reasons for your choice of the particular years, parts, or cases in your research plan. You must also consider whether your research will be sufficiently valid if you cannot visit a crucial archive and you have to rely on digital access. Are the digitalised collections preselected by the institutes that hold the archive? Which sources are made accessible and what can you not find online? In this same way, every source needs your careful consideration beforehand. You must outline a workable strategy for every research project, a strategy based on plausible considerations and arguments (see also Chapters 2 and 3).

1.4.2 Planning and feedback

planning

Your research plan obviously needs planning as well. Setting up and maintaining a sound schedule is of the greatest importance for every research project. Only by drawing up a schedule beforehand and considering it critically will it be revealed whether and how the initial research plan is achievable in the time available. For a Master's thesis, less time can be spent than on a doctoral thesis, on which a researcher has four years to work. The level of detail in the work plan depends on the size and duration of the research. Nevertheless, make an overall schedule for each relatively larger research project (such as a paper or a Master's thesis), indicating what needs to be done or expected interim results per month. Then, break it down into weekly or even daily work schedules.

While considering the time for actual research, remember the writing phases that will follow: make sure that you take the entire process into account.

When making such a schedule, your research and your writing will be divided into smaller parts. Carrying out research and writing an academic text is a complex procedure. Rarely is it a simple straightforward exercise. Writing is thinking and searching for the narrative. In the middle of the research project, almost all researchers have difficulty maintaining an overview of the whole project. Similarly, it is difficult to foresee beforehand which details must be elaborated in order to make the research or the argument at large come true. Moreover, it is very rare that a book, a Master's thesis, or even a paper can be written in one attempt. Therefore, it is sensible to divide your work into smaller parts. Dividing up your work into these smaller units that are marked out in your schedule will ensure that the whole is manageable and organised. Such a division of work in a schedule will make it clear whether the proposed research is feasible. *schedule*

However, drawing up a schedule is not enough, of course. Once you have started your research or writing, it is important to check whether the work you are doing accords with your plan. It can happen that some work can be done more quickly or requires far more time than planned. Not only is this relevant in adjusting your schedule during the research, it can also be instructive to see the difference between your original plans and the time taken to do certain parts of the work. In time, this experience will lead to a better understanding of the advantages and disadvantages of the methods followed and to more insight into how much time certain tasks require (think of reading a difficult manuscript, transcribing an interview, organising a numerical database, correcting an OCR [Optical Character Recognition] text, etc.). It will also teach you how to apply variation in your work – for instance, doing work that requires little concentration (such as entering data or formatting) when you are tired and doing tasks requiring a great deal of concentration (such as analysis, searching for connections and writing) when you are in top form. In this way, you also discover which tasks are easier or more difficult for you. *adjusting your schedule*

Give some concentrated thought to your own skills. After all, you do not only want to know about history, you want to write history. Doing this frequently and systematically evaluating your schedule and the progress of your research will enable you discover your strong and weak points and bear them in mind when making future research plans. If you notice that you are often too optimistic when planning, it is sensible to allocate more time to tasks than you are inclined to think they would need. Or you can allocate more time to specific parts that you know are *your own strong and weak points* going to take more time, such as editing a text or writing a conclusion (historians often have trouble with conclusions, see also Chapter 4). If you notice that you tend to work against a deadline, it would be useful to consider this in your plans. A good solution would be to set earlier deadlines of your own, such as showing a first version to a friend or fellow student well in advance. Do not ask them simply for encouragement but specifically for criticism.

interim check　　Such interim checks are not only good for the manageability of the research, they are also part of the research itself. Interim reports – in the form of a research report or a draft version of a chapter, for example – of-
feedback　　fer others the opportunity to give feedback. The comments of supervisors, experts, colleagues, or fellow students not only help to improve your final result but are an important aspect of writing history as a debate of the interpretation of the past. There is no need to sit cloistered at home with the intention of presenting a unique final result when it is ready, just waiting to see how it is received. Instead, share your findings and discuss the past; it will give you a more focused view of your subject and your research question and will make others excited about seeing your final result.

adjusting your　　It could happen that you must adjust your research because of new
research　　insights or because a question or sub-question is more difficult to answer than expected. Perhaps the research question or the research plan has to be changed in some way. Drastic adjustments to the research, however, can imply that much of your earlier work was done for nothing. That is why both the exploratory phase of setting up your research and revisiting your original research question is so important. If adjusting the research is unavoidable, a common solution is to explicitly change your research question or your approach. It is always sensible to ask the opinion of supervisors, advisers, and others about altering your research plan.

This first chapter discussed the historical research process in general terms – designating a subject, formulating a research question, and deciding on what types of question, splitting the question into sub-questions, exploring the state of the literature on the subject, considering approaches to the problem, available sources and methods for dealing with those sources, and finally planning and critical self-evaluation of the research process whereby you actively seek feedback. The next chapter will discuss the building blocks of historical research – literature and sources.

Notes

1   E. van Nederveen Meerkerk, *De draad in eigen handen. Vrouwen en loonarbeid in de Nederlandse textielnijverheid, 1581-1810* (Amsterdam 2007) 19.
2   *Ibidem*, 24.
3   Sofie De Langhe, Maja Mechant, and Isabelle Devos, 'Regionale verschillen in het leven van ongehuwde moeders op het platteland in de Zuidelijke Nederlanden, 1730-1846', *Tijdschrift voor Sociale en Economische Geschiedenis* 8 (2011) 2-28.

2 THE BUILDING BLOCKS OF THE HISTORICAL METHOD

Every research project begins with a search for information. Looking for and collecting information is not a haphazard occupation but should follow certain guidelines. In the first place, this is because your search strategy determines what you find and what you do not find. Second, you must be able to evaluate the information you find. How do you find relevant academic literature and how do you know where to find the right sources? Which search strategy is best for you to follow to find the information you need? This chapter will help as it deals with such questions, including the difference between sources and academic literature. We shall discuss the various types of academic literature so that you can obtain a good understanding of the material for which you are searching and the differences between literature and sources, and between academic and non-academic literature. In the second part of this chapter, we shall explore in more detail where and how you can find the literature and sources for your research.

2.1   Primary and secondary sources

In the previous chapter, you will have read that when formulating a research question, it is important to demonstrate that it is academically relevant. Often when you think of a question, you will not have the necessary knowledge of the present state of the historical debate on your chosen subject. There is also often a lack of background historical knowledge. Of course, this will change as you become more acquainted with various historical subjects, and more and more frequently you will be able to formulate your question from the debate. However, that will not be the case when you start out. You will be able to formulate a research question only after a preliminary exploration on the basis of which you can write a *status quaestionis*. See Chapter 1 for more details. The next step in your research is always to delve deeper into the subject: you should look for background literature and sources. Before we deal with search strategies that you can use to find the right literature and sources, we shall discuss the differences *differences between* between primary and secondary sources, which are also known as *primary and* sources and (secondary) literature. You will use these terms through- *secondary sources* out your course of study, so it is important to fully understand the difference between the two.

2.1.1 Primary sources: Originating from the context

primary sources

When historians speak of sources – as the most direct access to a histori-cal context, often also called *primary* sources – they mean every type of documentation that comes directly from the period that the historian is researching. It refers to material that forms the basis for their considera-tion of events, circumstances, and actors in the past. There are many sorts of sources in many shapes, sizes, and materials – textual, visual, three-di-mensional, landscape, physics, bio-medical, digital, mental, sensory – and this is far from being a complete summary. Historiography has the most experience with textual sources.

The basis of source criticism is the evaluation of the information from this source. Archaeologists have more experience with three-dimensional sources garnered from excavations, for example with geological informa-tion and bio-medical information from human remains. With the aid of media studies, cultural science studies, art history, and museology, source criticism has been developed for audio-visual and artistic sources and ob-jects. In the *e-Humanities*, historians work with and consider new sources of our present time – textual, visual, and/or audible – that exist in digital form. The digital character of these sources does not mean that they are everlasting or immutable. Digital sources are just as changeable as the strata of geological formation at a prehistoric excavation, the ink on the paper of a nineteenth-century document from an archive, or the interior of a church that was a victim of iconoclasm. No source is static, as all sources change with time: they age, fade, or alter structure.

changing relations

Moreover, the relation between the sources, the time period from which they come, and the time in which they are considered relevant are subject to constant change. For instance, decolonisation has had a huge impact on how sources are dealt with and how history is written, both in the former colonised areas, such as the Congo and Suriname, and former colonial powers, such as Belgium and the Netherlands. Not only have historical themes such as slavery and colonial violence been subject to increased interest, these themes have brought new questions and sources to light. In the same way, the increased interest after 1989 in the significance of the First World War for relations in the Balkans has given a new immediacy to the sources concerning Dutch neutrality during that war.

meaning is always ambiguous

Historians have access to many types of sources of which the meaning is never unambiguous. With every research question, it is important to really consider which sources can be used, what information can be found in these sources, and how information from various sources might be re-lated. We shall address the use of sources more fully later in this chapter.

2.1.2   Secondary sources: Academic historical literature

By secondary sources, we mean the whole gamut of academic publications that historians use to acquire the necessary background information and the theoretical and historiographical context. Historians often refer to this as 'literature'; in this case, the word means something rather different from when it is used to designate a literary text.

background and embedding

Secondary sources or literature are not completely distinct from primary sources. Certain secondary sources in one research project could be primary sources in another. For example, when a researcher asks how the question of Dutch slavery has been dealt with in the last hundred years in the works of other historians, the academic publications from the last century furnish the sources for this research. Non-academic publications, too – such as fiction; poetry; memoirs; travel books; photographic albums; collection catalogues of the work of artists, of museum collections, or other collections – can be either primary sources or literature, depending on the research question. To make that distinction clearer, literature is also called 'secondary literature'. In fact, that is redundant, but the repetition gives extra emphasis to the difference from primary sources as originating in a specific historical period.

2.2   Finding your way in academic historical literature

The first step to gaining a more thorough understanding of your subject is a search for academic publications that are important in that field. To search for literature in the right way and to evaluate properly what you find, it is important to be able to differentiate between various types of publications. The content and structure of a text is largely determined by the type of text. There is a huge difference between reading an article and reading a collection, a monograph, or a webpage. The type of text has a considerable impact on the text analysis that you conduct and the sort of information that you can gain from it.

publication types

The various types of publications also require their own forms of search techniques. Below, we provide a brief explanation of important types of academic publications, divided into (a) textbooks, (b) monographs, (c) collections, (d) journal articles, and (e) encyclopaedic works.

2.2.1 Literature of all types and lengths: From textbooks to journal articles

textbooks
(a) Textbooks. A textbook is used chiefly as an introduction to a certain field of history. History courses often start with a prescribed series of textbooks in the first year. A textbook gives a broad, coherent overview of a particular research area, with overviews of eras such as the medieval period and early modern history; however, they might focus on a specific theme such as religion, genocide, labour, sexuality, globalisation, or multicultural relations. Textbooks are usually written by a number of authors whose individual contribution to the text is not recognisable. They base their work chiefly on academic literature rather than on primary sources *synthesis* and attempt to sketch a synthesis in which the knowledge available is put into a larger narrative. A good textbook has an extensive bibliography. Textbooks are useful because they provide an overview of fields of history and set out all the important events and dates clearly, information that enables you to place your own research in a relevant historical framework. Moreover, they can be a source of inspiration for research themes.

(b) Monographs. A monograph is a book about a specific subject by a single author or group of authors who write the text. They differ from textbooks in that they often go into greater depth and are more specialised. A monograph is usually based on the author's own research in which *monograph* mostly primary sources are used. Monographs generally consist of an argument – in contrast to the usually descriptive character of textbooks. As your study progresses, you will make less use of textbooks and turn increasingly to monographs and other specialised academic publications. *dissertation* Monographs can be divided into subtypes. For instance, there are dissertations (doctoral theses), which are written with the author's specific aim to give depth to a particular subject and highlight its importance, which, if successful, leads to the granting of a doctorate (PhD). Another example *biography* is the biography, which is an academic or popular scientific description of someone's life. An autobiography – written by the subject him- or herself – is rarely an academic monograph and usually cannot be used as a secondary source.

Monographs can be the result of long-term research with no obvious larger interest or may be the result of a specific (short-term) commission. A monograph can present a theoretical view or go into a specific area of micro-history in the smallest detail. It can be an independent case study but have implications for comparable research, or it can be a comparative study with a larger common denominator of the various examples as its main theme. Like autobiographies, works that can be regarded as fiction, such as novels, poetry, film scenarios, and plays, cannot readily be considered monographs in the context of historical research.

(c) Collections. Various authors contribute to a collection. Collections are also called edited volumes. The most common types are conference collections (if the contributions to a conference are collected without extensive editing, they are known as 'proceedings' or conference reports), thematic collections, and 'Festschrifts' or commemorative collections. In a conference collection, the lectures and presentations that the participants have discussed at a particular conference are further elaborated upon and the discussions are incorporated into it, with the cooperation of the authors and editors of the collection. The editors of the collection often provide an introduction with a *status quaestionis* of the main theme and the specific contribution this collection hopes to make to the debate. Other collections more often represent a *status quaestionis* of a particular theme in a field and give an explicit explanation of this theme. The contributions aim to highlight various aspects and perspectives and stimulate discussion concerning the research agenda in that particular field. Finally, commemoration collections are usually put together for a particular occasion, such as a commemoration or jubilee, or to honour the work of a colleague who is about to retire.

thematic collection

Festschrift/ commemoration collection

In the context of your own research, you should often read such collections 'selectively'. Pay extra attention to the introduction, the bibliography, and the chapters that are relevant to your own research due to the subject or the author.

(d) Journal articles. In academic journals, individual authors publish (parts of) their own research. Historians publish in a wide range of journals: those dealing with the humanities, social sciences, popular scientific subjects, opinions, and so on.

academic journals

Some journals, such as *Past and Present*, cover a wide range of subjects and periods. Other historical journals are more specific, restricting themselves to a particular period or form. Examples of this type are *Journal of Global History*, *Sixteenth Century Journal*, and TSEG/*The Low Countries Journal of Social and Economic History*. Contributions to academic journals must go through various stages of review. They are evaluated by the editors for their suitability for the journal in question, and most journals then subject them to what is known as *peer review*. This means that other academics read the submissions and comment on them, usually anonymously. The editors decide, with the aid of those comments, whether the article should be published, either with or without revision. In the first place, this *peer review* functions as a guarantee of the quality of the articles: they ensure that the contributions meet the requirements for academic articles and also check for possible forms of plagiarism (see also Chapter 4). *Peer review* also contributes to the debate on ongoing historical research. Generally speaking, journal articles are the quickest form of

peer review

making ongoing research public. *The peer review* process allows research colleagues to become involved, and the research becomes implicitly – and after publication explicitly – embedded in a wider context.

As well as articles, most journals also publish reviews of (recent) books. In those reviews, an author – who is often an expert on the subject of the book – gives his or her judgement on the work and places the study in the context of contemporary research.

edited,
encyclopaedic, and
biographical works

reference works

digital
encyclopaedic works

(e) Encyclopaedic works. The types of historical publications discussed above can be found in either a printed or digital form and nowadays increasingly in both forms. This is also true of edited encyclopaedic and biographical works, atlases, dictionaries, and lexicons such as *Encyclopædia Britannica, Nieuw Nederlandsch Biografisch Woordenboek, Atlas bij de wereldgeschiedenis, Van Dale,* and *Digitaal Vrouwenlexicon van Nederland.* These 'traditional' historical reference works have editors who develop and approve the content provided by a great number of authors – often named – and are known to be 'factually reliable'. Such works aim to state the facts and incorporate as little interpretation as possible. They are still to be found in book form in most reading rooms. The majority of these reference works can also be found in digital form, and there are also new forms such as *Wikipedia* in which writing, editing and *peer review* is an interactive, collective undertaking. Digital encyclopaedic works increasingly serve as the first point of orientation on a subject and can help in acquiring more depth for a research question.

It is important to find out who is responsible for the information and to check its reliability (see also sections 2.2.3 and 2.2.4).

2.2.2   Search strategies for literature research

Now we come almost automatically to the most important aspect of this explanation of historical literature: how do you search this immeasurable amount of information? How can you filter it and make a selection from it? There are questions that can serve as guidelines to help you do this: Is there any relevant literature and what is it? How do I search this literature? How do I select the titles for my own research from the relevant literature? Libraries give all the publications in their collections a unique 'shelf mark', often a combination of letters and numbers that indicate where a publication is in the reading rooms or stacks. To ask for a book, you should use this number, which, as library collections are now automated, is linked to a barcode (which is also unique to both the collection and each publication). Since 1970, every work ever published has a unique number, its ISBN (International Standard Book Number). The ISBN contains information about the country of publication, the pub-

libraries
shelf mark

ISBN

lisher, and the number of the book given by the publisher. Journals have a unique number for the whole series, the ISSN (International Standard Series Number). These numbers are important for retailers and librar- *ISSN*
ies. However, unlike the unique numbers of objects in collections, as we shall see later, the researcher usually has little to do with them. Moreover, researchers are not only interested in officially published works but also in those from before the implementation of ISBN and what is called 'grey' *'grey' literature*
literature – reports, Master's theses, illegal publications, and so forth. Li-
braries also collect this grey literature.

The first means of access when searching for literature is an online *online (search)-* (search) catalogue. Many libraries have their own catalogues for the *catalogue*
printed books they hold and the *e-books* to which they can give access. Normally speaking, a library catalogue does not include articles. In addition, there are umbrella catalogues – in the Netherlands, the most important is *Picarta*, a national catalogue containing various sorts of *Picarta*
material. In this extremely extensive file, you will find books, journals, articles, abstracts, letters, sheet music, multimedia, and internet services. The catalogue offers access to both the collections in Dutch libraries and numerous databanks and journals. The advantages of a search in Picarta is that it includes journal articles and that a successful hit means that you can be certain that the book can be found somewhere in the Netherlands.

More and more university libraries (in Dutch, UBS) also use search en- *search-engines* gines/*discovery tools* that not only search their own collection but can also search worldwide. These search systems with names such as Primo and OCLC Worldcat often have their own name in the UBS, for example Smart-
cat at the UB Groningen University and Catalogus+ at the University of Amsterdam UB. With the arrival of these new search engines, which also search the collections of the major Dutch libraries, the importance of Picarta is likely to decrease. Via other catalogues, such as that of the *Library of Congress* in the USA, you may also come across titles that are essential for your research. For your research, you must also consult the titles that cannot be found in the university or municipal libraries clos-
est to you. Sometimes, you can do that by visiting another university or municipal library. University libraries and other major libraries also allow you to make use of inter-library loans (IBL) so that you can get publications from elsewhere. Moreover, many publications are available at the *Koninklijke Bibliotheek* (KB) in The Hague, whose task it is to collect and make available everything that is published in the Netherlands.

Library catalogues – like those of other institutes that hold collections such as museums and archives – are structured on the foundations of a long tradition of organising information. An important part of this is the evolution of the *thesaurus* as a system in which keywords – and therefore *thesaurus*
subjects – are connected to each other and put in order. A keyword is a

concept given to a publication by the cataloguer. It is not, therefore, the same thing as a title word or a concept that the author has expressed in the title of the publication. As a rule, it concerns what are known as *facet thesauri*. In general, a book deals with a number of subjects, places, or persons. A *facet thesaurus* offers search possibilities by way of various types of keywords: for example, by author, subject, period, and geographic area. Before the advent of computers, these search possibilities were stored in card indices: for each title there were various cards, one was alphabetically arranged by author, another by subject, a third by geographic area, and so on. With the advent of digital online catalogues and the *discovery tools* mentioned above, this system has become very refined, with increasing coordination of keywords, regardless of the language, so that it is now easier to make connections between various catalogues and databases.

To prevent you becoming lost in the plethora of hits, university libraries offer online exercise modules to teach you how to carry out a good search in the various catalogues using the advanced search options and filters.

filters   Filters offer the possibility of reducing the number of hits for a search. They are incorporated on the basis of what we call the *metadata* of each title (which is often linked to *facet thesauri*). They help to narrow down a wide search. To work with them efficiently, it is important that you deter-*search terms*   mine the relevant search terms, keywords, and codes of your subject. The *metadata*   keywords can generate hits in metadata (persons, periods, events, places) in the title of the relevant literature. Let's say you want to research the migration of French Huguenots to the Low Countries in the seventeenth century. It is sensible not to use 'Huguenots' as your only search term. If you do so, you will find information about Huguenots in France and other countries. In short, the search term here is far too broad. In this case, it would be useful to go to *advanced search* and combine various terms. Search for 'Huguenots' and 'Netherlands' and you will find much more relevant information that you can then filter further for such aspects as period.

codes   Libraries and other institutions use codes to standardise the placing of publications and subjects, often by thematic, regional, or temporal division into subfields. The codes of the Nederlandse Basisclassificatie (NBC) [Dutch Basic Classification], for instance, indicate the discipline and subdiscipline to which a subject belongs. Depending on your subject and research question, such codes can also be used to search for relevant and related publications. A code can offer a handhold, but it is almost never enough for your search for information. Moreover, the Dutch Basic Classification is somewhat lacking in refinement. Studies that touch on the history of the Huguenots in the Netherlands might be covered by code '15.70' (History of Europe) and by '11.55' (Protestantism). Therefore, it might be important to use other standardised codes and keywords too (which can be found with the help of the titles you have already found in the library catalogue, for example). In that case, bear the following points in mind:

- Before you start your search, see which keywords and/or codes are used in the collection you are searching.
- Think of various synonyms for your search terms. For example, the *synonyms* Netherlands in the early modern period is often called the Republic. You cannot assume that the link will always be made automatically. So always use several search terms.
- It is important not only to be aware of synonyms. In the example above, we called the Huguenots migrants. They were also described as *interpretative* religious refugees. Bear in mind the various interpretive frameworks *frameworks* when considering your search terms.
- Formulate keywords in other languages too. English is a particularly *other languages* important academic language. For specific themes, it can be useful and important to search for literature in another modern language. Not all library systems have a translation programme that automatically enlarges the area of your search by translating the terms.

2.2.3 Looking further

Once you have found a few works, you can use the following methods to find more literature.

1. **The snowball method.** This method refers to the process of *snowball method* searching through footnotes and bibliographies of books you have already found. Because the literature you already have is used to find more literature, the snowball method means that the references to relevant *literature references* studies will increase, providing you with an efficient means of accessing a very broad pool of literature. However, there are disadvantages to this method. First, the bibliographical references in a particular study reflect the author's research and selection, and consequently there is a risk that you could miss important literature. You might also be snowed under with detailed information. Certain information might have been important for the author in question but is perhaps less significant for your own research.

Moreover, if you confine yourself to the notes and literary references in a publication, the snowball method is like a rear-view mirror: it only includes the titles that were available when the work in which they were listed was published. In the Arts and Humanities Citation Index (part of the Web of Science), you can 'snowball' both backwards and forwards. The index lists the works that the publications included in it cite and where the publication itself has been cited. Be aware of the limitations of this method as regards older publications: with this method you could easily miss new works and earlier conclusions might have been criticised in later publications.

publication lists

2. **Big names.** When you know which scholars are important in the field of your research subject, it is advisable to check a list of their publications. Most scholars have an up-to-date bibliography on their personal websites. You can also search catalogues for the authors' names. This will often allow you to find more references to their work, and once you have the publications, you can apply the snowball method again. Moreover, this method will help you become up to date with the latest developments.

historiographical overviews

3. **Historiography.** In most monographs, and to lesser degree in collections and journals, the author gives an explanation of the state of research concerning the subject. These historiographical overviews (*status quaestionis*) offer a good way of finding out what literature is important for a theme. It is important to remember, however, that the author's analysis cannot be accepted without question. First study the relevant works: it is quite possible that this will lead to a different analysis of the literature or the meaning of a particular author. Perhaps the overview lacks an important work. Comparing various historiographical overviews helps to prevent such pitfalls.

journal articles

reviews

4. **Searching journals.** Research-in-progress is often published in journals, which means that journal articles present the latest state of research in a field. By this, we do not just mean articles about a specific subject: journals also publish discussion dossiers, polemics, and reviews. In this respect, the reviews in such journals as BMGN – *Low Countries Historical Review, Tijdschrift voor Geschiedenis* and *Nieuwe West-Indische Gids*, book sections of daily and weekly magazines, and *The New York Review of Books* can be very helpful.

It is always advisable to look at the most recent issues of the influential journals in your research area to see if any relevant articles have been published. The German *Recensio.net, review platform for European history* has an extended search engine and provides ample access to digitally available reviews in dozens of European historical journals. The same applies to the Arts and Humanities Citation Index (part of the Web of Science) we mentioned above.

5. **Google Scholar, Web of Knowledge, JSTOR, Muse, World-Cat, and other places for digital searches.** From what we have already said, it should be clear that with the advent of the digital era the search options for every (prospective) historian have increased enor-

mously. The access to digital databases, virtual libraries, and automated catalogues make it increasingly easier to find literature. Two important digital libraries are JSTOR and Muse. These institutions cooperate with a great many libraries and publishers to make journals and other digital publications accessible. Other frequently used digital literary collections are Google Scholar and Google Books. Both generate titles and (parts of) publications, reviews of works, and information about other authors who have used the work in question. If you use Google Books, you will frequently discover that not all the digital work is available due to copyright laws. By using keywords, you can still often search the book or article – and therefore not just at the level of the title or the *metadata* linked by libraries. A large database for digitalised books in the Netherlands is DBNL – *Digitale Bibliotheek voor de Nederlandse Letteren*.

digital databases, virtual libraries

Google Books

DBNL

With such book collections, you may be tempted – more so than with articles, which can be downloaded and printed faster – to look only for passages that can be used for your research. In a scholarly sense, that is not advisable. Become thoroughly acquainted with a book, even when it is in digital form, and concentrate on the author's arguments, on the choice of sources, and on the nature of the debate of which the book is part. Only then can you really evaluate the information that you gain from it for your own research.

the entire book

6. Bibliographical aids. Finally, always search through the Historical Abstracts database and look at the available (digital) bibliographies. Historical Abstracts is a very extensive historical database – going back to 1953 and in some cases still further – with a sophisticated system of filters that makes it possible to search in thousands of historical journals for subject, author, period, etc. The *Digitale Bibliografie Nederlandse Geschiedenis* (DBNG), the International Medieval Bibliography, and the Arts and Humanities Citation Index (Web of Science) are also important.

Historical Abstracts

In addition to these databases, specialised bibliographies can be useful as they give an overview of publications on a particular theme, field, or author. Accordingly, you can find works that are not (or no longer) in libraries and thus do not appear in online catalogues. In this digital age, printed bibliographies are seldom published. Thanks to the extensive digital search options, they are simply no longer profitable and quickly become out of date. The bibliographies that are still produced are put online and can be found on the websites of research projects, educational establishments, or (popular) scientific websites, such as www.vijfeeuwenmigratie.nl. When using a bibliography, it is always important to note the publication date: when was the bibliography completed and when was it last updated? Of course, this also holds true for online bibliographies.

bibliographies

2.2.4 Consider your search results

When you are using (online) aids for research, these sorts of considerations and know-how are important. Often they are related to what is *media awareness* called digital or academic 'media awareness'. None of the search strategies we have discussed provides on its own a full overview of the available literature. Behind all the catalogues and search engines, there is a hidden history of collecting, selecting, and choices for digitisation. For instance, when you use the snowball method, the result will always be limited by the choices of the author in question. Someone who does not know German usually ignores literature in that language. Similar limitations also apply to digital libraries such as JSTOR or Muse: if a journal is not part of the group, the articles in that journal cannot be found by their search engines. Moreover, digital search engines work with statistical procedures by which a hit of 99 percent turns up higher in the search results than a partial hit of, say, 40 percent. In this way, the search engine 'learns', or is programmed to remember, which outcome is most frequently accepted as a result. The search engine often even takes into consideration the location of the computer conducting the search – what country, institution, and postcode. In addition, other interests can also play a role. For example, research institutes can manage the registering of what are called 'impact scores' of researchers that are related to the question of how frequently a work is consulted and cited. This can lead to the stimulus to give certain search results priority. This does not mean that they have suddenly become bad search results, but it is just as likely that information that is important for you but is less 'prominent' will be ignored.

research context It is also important to realise that every catalogue and search engine is embedded in a certain research context. Some search engines deal primarily with the humanities, while others serve the exact sciences. This *selection mechanisms* determines the selection mechanism of the search engine. There are differences not only between specific disciplines but also between national research traditions that play a role here. For instance, if you are researching a French, Italian, or German subject, you cannot always use the catalogues mentioned above. For example, Google Books is strongly orientated towards English-language books and has little literature in German or other languages, nor will you find all Italian journals in something like JSTOR.

It is therefore necessary to use not just one search method but several methods together to complement each other when searching for literature. Consider, too, that you must not embark on an endless search and that you should initially limit yourself to the authoritative literature in order to find a direction.

2.3   Orientation on primary sources: Can everything be a source?

Good historical research is more than processing literature: it is original work, and the analyses are based on the interpretation of sources that embody a relationship with earlier times. The history researcher is looking for new insights, and to find them you must go back to source material that has information about the subject and the period that you are researching. Compared to looking for good literature, finding the right sources is a huge challenge. In this section, we will discuss the points to bear in mind when searching for sources. What are good search strategies and what are the pitfalls? To explain these, it is necessary to consider the various types of sources used by historians in more detail. Here, they are *types of sources* briefly summarised and divided into textual, visual, material, and auditory (including *oral history*) sources.

2.3.1   Sources in all shapes and sizes: From text to image and sound

The differentiation in this division is not absolute but primarily concerns the sort of information for which the source is examined. After all, a piece *information* of paper with writing on it is not only a 'text' but also a 'thing' – a piece of paper manufactured and written on during a certain time period and using a certain technique. The same is true of photographs, which are not just 'images' but also objects, made and distributed according to certain techniques. There are also objects that frequently contain text, which is part of their meaning – think of coins. *meaning*

The material aspect of primary sources is part of what is known as 'source criticism' – the interpretation of the source. Historical research has long been dominated by the importance of texts. Interviews can only *text* be a historical source that can be checked if they are recorded in texts (notes, transcriptions), by audio recordings, or in moving images. Historians can often only work with objects if there is textual documentation – written on the back, a caption in an album, a vignette of a photograph as an indication as to how the photograph should be understood.

In this regard, historical research has a different emphasis than, say, archaeological or art historical research. Nevertheless, historians are conscious of the interaction between the textual, material, and visual aspects *relation between* of their sources. The way in which historians can access sources contains *historians and their* what is called performative capacity: the characteristics of the source play *source material* a role in the relation between historians and their source material. Some sources are more obvious than others. Some seem more convincing because they are neatly organised, while others are impressive because of where they were found. Some are special because of their aroma, while others are vulnerable because of their fragile state, and so on. Sources also have a time dimension. For example, it can take hours to read a difficult manuscript or two hours to watch a film. In both cases, you can see the information medium – the manuscript or the roll of film – in a moment, but it renders its information only when the time is taken to read or watch it. A similar exploration of archives also influences the historian. This performative effect varies from person to person – and historians are as diverse as the sources. The rules of the discipline demand that the information and experiences of source examination in historical research are handled in such a way that they can be recognised and checked by *types of sources* colleagues. The division into the four types of sources – (a) written, (b) material, (c) visual, and (d) auditory (oral communication, sound recording) – can help with this. Moreover, today, we have to deal with a fifth type of source: sources of digital origin for each genre.

textual sources   (a) **Textual sources** can be divided into numerous different types – ledger accounts, literary texts, ego documents, pamphlets, minutes, reports, identity papers, etc. There are too many to summarise all the possible types, but what they have in common is that their importance for their makers lies, in the first place, in the written information they contain. Because of the emphasis on what is written in them and the historical context of that content, they are often regarded as 'two-dimensional' information carriers, in other words, as flat surfaces. Written sources can be found everywhere. The most important historically organised holdings of written sources are 'archives' – which will be discussed later. It is important that the same text can be found in different places and sometimes in more than one archive – as a carbon copy, a digital copy, or because it is a printed source. Therefore, the finding places of written sources and the context in which they were preserved is always relevant.

material sources   (b) **Material sources** can be of natural origin or man-made, varying from ornamentation to utensils and from unique craft objects to mass-produced machine products. With respect to material sources, the three-dimensional aspect is of prime importance. The historian attempts to 'read' historical information from their physical characteristics in combination with the information about where they come from (*provenance*). Material sources can be found everywhere too, and they also do not need to be unique. The most important historically organised holdings are (museum) depots, although libraries and archives sometimes have surprising collections of material culture. The Vrije Universiteit Amsterdam, for example, has in its collection the furniture and death mask of Abraham Kuyper, and every library has its attic full of odds and ends.

(c) **Visual sources** were primarily made to show something that must *visual sources* be understood as an image. Visual sources can be two- or three-dimensional – sculptures, paintings, photographs – and they too can have a specific relation to time. We can distinguish between visual arts, photography, and film according to their aspects of uniqueness or reproducibility. Every single painting by Rembrandt is unique. A print of a photograph printed by Eva Besnyö herself in a limited edition (*vintage print*) *unique or in edition* is 'authentic' as an object. However, the image might have also become historically relevant because it can be found in several places and in different forms. The photograph might be found in a coarse-grained format in the newspaper that printed it as a news photograph or as a *vintage print* in the collections of various museums that managed to obtain a copy. The images of both a photograph and a painting can be reduced in size and brought onto the market as a postcard. Many of these images can be research material for historians – think of posters or advertisements, such as the *Verkade albums*. The collection traditions for photographs and comparable types of sources are much younger than those for written sources, visual arts, and material culture. This is due not only to the fact that the techniques are much newer but also because, for a long time, photographs were seen as 'snapshots' of a time. Nevertheless they have been widely collected in newspaper archives, museum collections, print rooms, and the picture collections of libraries and archives.

(d) **Auditory sources**, particularly **oral records**, are transient if the narratives, reminiscences, structured interviews, and other forms of conversation are not captured in written form or on audio or visual data carriers. Such oral sources, more commonly than other sources, are *oral sources* formed during the process of writing history. Written, visual, and material sources usually exist before the historical study. In the case of oral sources, the historian him- or herself 'makes' sources by going to people and posing questions or observing and making notes about how people speak about the subject as an anthropologist does. The professional practices connected to the preservation of these sources and to their availability to third parties are still being developed. The Data Archiving and Networked Services (DANS) institute, which in the Netherlands is concerned with archiving digital research data such as databases, also deals with the storage and management of interviews and digital audio files. In addition, specialised archives and museum collections are increasingly able to conserve these sources or even to proactively create them. One example of this is the Institute for Women's History Atria (previously known as Aletta), which conducted interviews with women who were active in the Netherlands in the communist resistance to the Nazi occupation and with the children of parents who were Nazi sympathisers *listen or read*

during the same period. Consulting such oral sources – as they are accessible – demands of the historian a well-thought-through choice concerning the inherent time dimension of the source: to listen/watch or to read the transcript. The source does not only contain information about the events of the period, but also about what the narrative itself means. Body language, for instance, can say a great deal but is not easily transferred onto a paper transcript of an interview.

digital sources

(e) A final remark about **digital sources**. Digital sources are primary sources that come from the use of ICT and only exist in digital form (*born digital*). Meanwhile, many organisations (whether governmental or private) have made their whole administration digital; formerly, action groups 'once' made posters and pamphlets, whereas now, they work with *banners* and other digital means of action. Digital sources are breaking down the distinctions between written, material, visual, and auditory sources. Historical sources that exist only in digital format are built up of bits and bytes that can be in the form of a text, an image, or sound and can be sent to printers in an endless edition and in just about every imaginable format as a two- or three-dimensional copy to be further disseminated beyond the computer. For historians, important digital primary sources are, for example, websites or information collected from what is termed *social media*.

Libraries, archives, and other holders of collections must continually adapt to the demands concerning the archiving of the sources and long-term access to them. The successive changes in programming software for the production of, and access to, this digital data are creating a particular and very specialised problem. The obsolescence of older software and apparatus is a particular challenge. Other problems are connected with storage organisation and the selection of the endless amounts of digital data. It is exciting for historians to partake in this process of developing these new sources and standardising their storage and to be able to make a contribution to it by throwing research questions at the academics and managers who expand this technology even further.

2.3.2   Interaction between sources and interpretation

Diagram 1:
Diversity of sources
and interaction

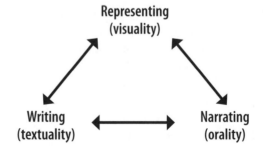

Now that all the types of sources, their various dimensions, and their per-formative aspects have been discussed, it will be obvious that experience of the whole range of sources will influence the way you work with one type of source. Perhaps someone who has considered body language in oral history will ask if the effect of body language on political debate can be found in the proceedings of the Lower House. Someone who is con-scious of the effect of time in film might read an account of a journey on foot in the sixteenth century with another idea of the significance of time as an aspect of distance. It is not only our present-day analysis of various types of sources that influences the totality of sources. Diagram 1 shows that when they were made, written, oral, and visual representations also influenced each other. There is a constant interaction between sources – between what is seen, told, read, depicted, discussed, and recorded. Con-sidering this interaction retrospectively is necessarily selective, and the historian chooses his or her own focus. To prevent the historian from los-ing all sense of direction when conducting research, certain steps should be taken. The following chapter therefore will deal with the organisation of research material. Before source material can be studied and organised, however, it first must be found.

interaction between sources

2.3.3 Access to collections of sources

Where you find sources that you will eventually use for research depends entirely on the type of source. Since there is an enormous variety, it is impossible to consider here the location of every source or every search strategy. To begin with, we will describe a few characteristics of the most important and widely used source collections and the way they are or-ganised in (a) archives, (b) published sources, (c) specialised historical databases, and (d) museum depots.

finding sources and search strategies

(a) **Archives.** The archive is the traditional field in which the histo-rian works. An archive is an institution that houses a 'collection of docu-ments, registers, audio media, records etc. from the past that one must or wishes to preserve', according to the *Van Dale* dictionary. In addition to archives managed by the government, there are many private institutions that manage archives. In common parlance, the word archive in the first place means the building, institution, or even the room or cupboard in which the documents are kept, but archivists use the word to indicate a cohesive collection of documents. The library of Leiden University has an archive with the academic notes and correspondence of the historian Johan Huizinga, and the archive of former prime minister Hendrikus Colijn can be found in the Historical Documentation Centre for Dutch Protestantism (1800-present) of the Vrije Universiteit Amsterdam. *Van*

Dale's definition mentions the obligation to archive and so refers to the Public Records Act in which the conditions and duties concerning the preservation of government archives are laid down.

archives The idea of archives is old. Church archives, family archives, the archives of the regional water management authorities (also referred to as water boards), and university archives can go back to early modern times or even earlier. The greatest shift in the area of archiving dates from the period of the French Revolution and Napoleon. Since then, the relationship between statehood and archiving has been considerably reinforced. A more recent expression of this is the division of the archives of the Dutch Antilles after 2010, when Curaçao and St. Martin became independent countries within the Kingdom of the Netherlands. As happened earlier with Aruba, the archives of Curaçao and St. Martin were split from those of the islands of Bonaire, St. Eustatius, and Saba, which chose to have the status of Dutch municipalities. Another example is the Suriname colonial archives: for a long time these were held in the Netherlands, but they have recently been returned to Suriname.

National Archive Archives can be roughly divided into four types. First, there are the national government archives such as the National Archive in The Hague (known until 2002 as the General State Archive), the National Archive Suriname in Paramaribo, or the General State Archive (*Archives de l'État*) in Brussels. Archives such as those mentioned above keep the archive material of central or national government bodies, along with material of national importance. For instance, in the National Archive in The Hague, there are also archives of important social organisations and individuals. The abbreviations used for state archives can change. Until 2002, the abbreviation for the National Archive in The Hague was ARA (*Algemeen Rijksarchief*); at present, the abbreviation NA (*Nationaal Archief*) is generally used.

regional historical centre As well as the central government archives, there are also state archives with a provincial function. In the Netherlands, every provincial capital (with the exception of The Hague) has a regional historical centre (RHC). These centres manage the archives of the province and other institutions (both state and private) that work at the provincial level. They also hold the local archives of municipalities and water boards that no longer operate independently. In Belgium, in addition to the General State Archive, the Royal Palace Archive, and the General State Archive 2 (including judicial archives), there are sixteen state archives that hold mostly provincial or regional (governmental) archives.

state archives

town, municipality, and district archives The third type of archive includes town, municipality, or district archives. These manage documents at the local level such as documents of the town council, guild archives, and the local birth, marriage and death registers.

Last but not least, there are numerous archives that cannot easily be put into a national, regional, or local category. For example, businesses keep their own archives, the Dutch royal house has its own archive, and other families sometimes keep (parts of) the family archive under their own control. In addition, there are many private archives and research institutions that are specialised in specific themes. An example of this is the International Institute for Social History in Amsterdam that conducts research but also manages archives related to the global history of social and political movements, such as the archives of trade unions and international organisations like Greenpeace. Finally, there are international archives such as that of the European Union or the United Nations. In many cases, archives are split up, with the older parts closed and transferred to an archive management body while the 'current' archive is held by an institution, political party, business, or other archiving body so that it is available for consultation.

business archives

family archives

international archives

Not all archives are accessible to the public. With respect to state archives, the length of the limited access to their archive material and the conditions under which it is accessible are regulated by law. To access private archives, you might need to obtain the permission of the institute controlling the archive, the title-holders, or surviving relatives.

accessibility

Which archive you should consult depends entirely on your research question: the division above into national, regional, and local is helpful. If you are researching the position of widows in the clothmakers' guild in Amsterdam in the eighteenth century, you obviously do not need to look for material in the city archives of Leiden. It is also possible that the research requires that you consult several archives. Perhaps you want to compare the grain porters' guild in Amsterdam with that of Antwerp. In that case, you will need to search both archives for the right sources. Of course, your choice of archive is also determined by the presence of certain sources, but how do you find out what there is – and what is missing – in an archive? In order to know which collections are held in a particular archive it is advisable to first consult the summary of the collection. In most cases, archives have made such overviews accessible on their own website. An overview of the various archives, chiefly in the Netherlands and Flanders, can be found at www.archiefnet.nl. Other archive overviews are often thematic, such as that of private archives in Flanders and Brussels in *Archiefbank* (www.archiefbank.be) or the worldwide summary of archive material of the Verenigde Oost-Indische Compagnie [Dutch East India Company] (http://databases.tanap.net/vocrecords/). Such overviews can help to locate archival sources for research.

overview of archives

A collection summary is not enough to acquire more information about the specific items you might be able to use. You will need to use the inventory of the archive in question. An inventory is a systematic

inventory

description of the various parts of the collection of an archive, numbered according to those parts. In most cases, the inventory includes an introduction to the specific archive (for example, a brief history of its organisation), a description of the items, and an index. The descriptions of the items are the most important when you are looking for the right sources.

To explain how to work with an inventory, we will take as an example the archive of the Council of State between 1581 and 1795 in the National Archive in The Hague. This archive is divided into seven themes: (1) Resolutions, records, and reports, (2) The Union and further Union, (3) Land Defence, (4) Finances of the Generality, (5) Administration and governance of the Generality Lands, (6) Military and Generality Legal Decisions, and (7) Archive maintenance. In many cases, the separate parts are divided up and identified by their own numbers or letters. So under the heading *Resolutions, records, and reports*, you will find a separate heading for *resolutions*, a separate heading for *incoming post*, another heading for *outgoing post*, and so on.

online search portal

Nowadays, most archives have put their inventories online and they are digitally searchable, making it possible to search for archive items using keywords or names. Almost all archives have their own online search portal, and this makes it easy to search all the archives in, say, the National Archive or the City Archives of Rotterdam. A general search portal for Dutch archives can be found at www.archieven.nl; it is managed by a firm dealing in archiving systems. Such general search portals can contain out-of-date information, so it is better to consult the inventory and other information provided by the institution holding the archive in question. Moreover, it is important to remember that the digital search

limitations

of archive inventories has severe limitations. A digital search will only render items for which the search term has been used in the inventory. Archive inventories are almost never so detailed that present-day search terms are a good match for the contents of archive items. Consequently, it is possible that a search using your search terms finds nothing even though there may be relevant sources in that particular archive. Therefore it is always advisable to read through the inventory of possibly relevant archives yourself. This will not only provide insight into the content and structure of the archive but will often lead to new ideas for usable sources.

research guides

Many institutions publish research guides that serve as manuals for researchers. These research guides have a specific theme as their focus, such as the research guide to social security between 1890 and 1967 by the Huygens Institute for Dutch History (Huygens ING), the online guides *Plantages in Suriname* [*Plantations in Suriname*] and *Voorouders in slavernij in Suriname* [*Ancestors in Slavery*] on the website of the National Archive in The Hague, and the guide to genealogical research for Moluccan or

Moroccan ancestors by the Dutch Central Bureau for Genealogy. Such research guides chart the sources and the archives to which they belong. In addition, they often give background information, including information about the institutions from which the sources come. In the past, the tasks of various governmental bodies were not always clearly defined. In such cases, the research guides can be aids in administrative history. However, here too, it is advisable not to limit yourself to the information offered by the research guides. Although the intention of the editors is to serve as broad a public as possible, it is possible that your specific research question is not covered by the framework of the research guide. So always look for the sources yourself!

(b) Published sources. It is not necessary to go to an archive for your research in every case. Sometimes, published sources are sufficient. From the nineteenth century onwards, historians began producing editions of sources because many archives were difficult to access or the items were fragile and/or difficult to read. To make these documents accessible to researchers, they began to transcribe the texts of important sources and set these in publications of sources. The best-known of these published sources in the Netherlands is the series *Rijks Geschiedkundige Publicatiën* [*State Historical Publications*]. As mentioned earlier, many of these published sources are now available online. Before you use a published source, it is necessary to find out how academic it is – and thereby its degree of reliability. An academic source publication not only has a good transcription but also an accurate description of the original, the place it is held, and the reasons for publishing the source edition. From these publications, you can easily trace the original document, for instance, if you want to know if there are other texts or items in that archive that would be relevant for your research but have not been included in the published edition. In this context, it is important to make a distinction between a source edition and a digitally available source. In the first case, it is a transcription of the original; in the second, it is a scan of the original. A scan that allows you to see the original is not necessarily more reliable than the transcription. If the context in which the scan was made and placed online is not clearly given, the source is virtually unusable. It is advisable not to use a source without justification or context. For example, Canadian veterans of the Second World War have placed all sorts of documents concerning the course of the war and the activities of their regiments on their website. The documents come from far and wide and make an interesting digital collection. However, often their annotation is not satisfactory and so their origin (*provenance*) and the selection methods used are unclear. This means that the website as a 'published source' is unreliable, but at the same time it is an interesting primary source

published sources

reliability

provenance

for discussions among Canadian veterans about their part in the Second World War.

(c) **Databases.** With the advent of the digital era, many individual historians and specialised institutes have recorded information from sources *databases* in databases using software such as Excel or Access. In most cases, this is serial numerical data collected by doing quantitative and statistical analyses with the help of the database. These databases include information that comes from historical sources, but that does not mean that all the information from the source is included in the database. Often, it is *specific selection of* a specific selection of information. The selection might be influenced by *information* the possibilities of the source itself but also the purpose of the research and the available means such as time, funding, and manpower. An example of a source that is particularly suitable to record in a database, is the 'block books' (*Blokboeken*) of the city of 's-Hertogenbosch. In the second half of the eighteenth century, these books registered the city's population to prevent people coming from outside the city of becoming too great a burden on the city's poor relief fund. The 'block books' listed all the heads of the families in the city, including their professions, addresses, the size of their families, and the assistance they received from the poor relief fund or other charities. Because this information has been entered into a database, researchers can access all sorts of information about the socio-economic composition of the citizens of 's-Hertogenbosch in the eighteenth century.

sorts of databases Roughly speaking, there are two sorts of databases: (1) databases set up by a historian for his or her own research, and (2) those set up as part of a project or by an institute without a specific research project in mind but intended to serve as many historians as possible.

The first sort of database has something of a 'personal' character: the researcher has often spent a great deal of time collecting, entering, and processing the data with a specific goal in mind. Obviously, many historians are not always prepared to make those databases available as basic research data to third parties, certainly when they intend to use the information in the database for publications. Nonetheless, there are many others that are prepared to do so. Once again, a distinction must be made between making a database available for 'open access' and making it available to friends and colleagues. In the first case, it is available to anyone interested. In the Netherlands, numerous databases have been made accessible in this way via DANS (Data Archiving and Networked Systems) from the Koninklijke Nederlandse Akademie der Wetenschappen [Royal Academy of Arts and Sciences] (KNAW). In the second case, it depends on the researcher's personal favour if he or she is willing to send you the database. In both cases, it is important to look at the context in which the database was created and the degree to which you yourself can extract new information from it. After all, the maker has made the collection with a specific research question in mind. Has he or she omitted any information that would be useful for you? How has the research question influenced the structure of the database?

With respect to the second sort of database, set up by a larger project or an institution, the aim is to make as much information as possible available to as many researchers as possible. In many cases, such databases are available via 'open access'. With 'linked open data', they are also often connected with other relevant databases, such as that of Statistics Netherlands. In some cases, the researcher must ask permission for access on the grounds of his or her research proposal. To gain insight into the information available in such public databases and how they are put together, it is always important to look at the background of the project or the institute. Moreover, it is important to know how a project is financed. Which research group or institution is behind it, and how does this influence the information available? Is it current research whereby the database will change, or is the project finished and is the information in the database fixed? How durable is the access to the database – is there institutional embedding? In recent years, major online databases *online database* have been developed such as the *Historische Steekproef Nederland [His-* *projects* *torical Sample of the Netherlands]* and the *Global Collaboratory on the History of Labour Relations* by the International Institute for Social History. Some databases have a public function as well as a research function. The National Archive has a website where visitors can access databases like voc *Opvarenden* (listing all passengers and crew members on board of voc ships), *Vrijgelaten Slaven en Eigenaren* (providing information about *freed slaves and* their *owners*), and *Hindostaanse Immigranten in Suriname* (about contract labourers of Indian descent in Suriname).

There have been many developments in recent years when it comes to qualitative digital data sets, for instance with the aid of semantic web technology or other programmes and infrastructures. As with quantita- *quantitative and* tive databases, it is necessary to know more about the organisation of the *textual databases* data and the formulation of *Queries*. These new textual databases require insight into the programming language and corresponding programming questions. At this point, it are mainly computer scientists and linguists that deal with the forming of codes and calculations that facilitate processing on textual databases and not so much historians. However, the evident significance of such databases as collections of primary textual sources and the expected blurring of the division between digitised archives and *born digital archives* will require of historians that they, too, master these new techniques of data interpretation. Only historians can *data-interpretation* formulate the relevant historical questions that can lead the developments in the field of historical sources in a fruitful direction.

(d) Documentation of museum collections. By far the most important access to systematically collected material and visual primary sources are the systems of documentation which museums use for their collection. Like libraries, museums work with catalogues, and as with libraries and archives, all pieces in a museum have a unique collection number. In many cases, this goes back to the acquisitions book in which new acquisitions are inscribed according to date. Similar to shelf marks of library books, collection numbers are often composed of a combination of letters and numbers, whereby the letters indicate a specific part of the collection. In the Rijksmuseum in Amsterdam, 'kog' followed by a number refers to the collection of the Koninklijk Oudheidkundig Genootschap [Royal Antiquarian Society]. 'A' in the collection of the Tropenmuseum [Museum of the Tropics] in Amsterdam stands for the collection of Artis [the Amsterdam zoo]. Museums also often use the principle of serial numbers. The pieces from one collector, for example, all have the same number, expanded by a second sequence number. In the Rijksmuseum Volkenkunde [National Museum of Ethnology] in Leiden, all the pieces from the Royal Curiosities Cabinet, which existed between 1816 and 1883, have the serial number 360, followed by a sequence number. When museums enter their collections into a digital documentation system, all the objects are given a unique barcode as a number. The relation to the original unique number remains intact because the historical information is attached to that number.

museums' collection documentation systems

collection numbers

object information Traditional museum documentation recorded important information (if available) related to the date of acquisition, from whom and how it was acquired, the geographical origin, the maker, the object's age, the material, the function, and other information about its use. Because photography did not exist, or was uncommon in the documentation system, the original object documentation also often contains a detailed description of the appearance of the object. In these descriptions, documenters often used their own jargon for decoration, materials, and traces of use and wear. Often, the documentation of the collection also includes references about the use of objects in exhibitions, their restoration history, and any publication in which the object was mentioned. An increasing number of museums include part of this information in digital collection databases. Sometimes, the database contains no more than the 'basic registration'. The main information about the object is given as metadata, usually including a short title or description. However, the researcher can often ask for access to a more extensive version of the same database or to the original 'analogue' documentation system to obtain more background information about the object. Importantly, these digital databases have two- or three-dimensional digital images of many objects, photographs, and paintings. Sometimes, the original description cards are available available as a scanned image.

collection database

background information

The access to museum collections is organised in different ways based on the perspectives of the various disciplines. Art history still relies heavily on what is called the ICONCLASS system, which is a classification system that is linked to iconographic thesauri, and enables a systematic division of different types of art works and images. Folklore and ethnographic collections tended to use the UDC system (Universal Decimal Classification), which is also used as the basis for the organisation of many library collections and which allowed for an advanced state of refinement in terms of geographical origin, function, and material. Knowledge of these systems is still relevant because they also give an indication of the collection categories and the processes of attributing significance to them in the past. They show what the collectors wanted to know about the collections and consequently, indirectly, what other possible significance was subordinate to that. A topical example is the search for objects related to slavery in Dutch history. An analysis of earlier classification categories helps in the search for what was *not* catalogued as such at the time.

ICONCLASS

UDC

classification categories

The importance of this is also clear when you consult combined museum collections, such as in EUROPEANA. This portal to collections residing in a great number of museums, archives, and libraries is searchable for hits at the level of metadata. Once you have a set of hits, you can click on each item for the database of the institution in which that particular item can be found. For instance, you can search for everything about the Eiffel Tower or the First World War or the Dutch Queen Wilhelmina. In the case of the Eiffel Tower, it could be a historical collection based on the World Exhibition of 1889, an art collection with cityscapes of Paris, or a political item from a television news broadcast in which the reporter chose the Eiffel Tower as a background. Each item is consequently stored in a different collection context that gives the subject significance.

EUROPEANA

Now we have dealt with the difference between primary sources and secondary literature, and the diversity of primary sources and their embedding in various academic disciplines and collecting traditions, and we have given a brief idea of how you can come across these in libraries, archives, and museums. It is important information but it will only really come to life when you start to do research yourself, which is what we shall address in the next chapter.

3 APPLYING THE HISTORICAL METHOD

Now that you know where you can find literature and sources and how you should approach them, we will consider more fully how you can organise the information and do research. First of all, historical research is an incremental process. You cannot begin to write until you have obtained the information. If you do so, you run the danger of working selectively and, for instance, searching only for information that accords with what you want to say. Research means asking questions and being ready to accept unexpected answers. It is a process in which research plans and questions must be constantly adjusted in accordance with the (interim) results of the research. Therefore, it is also important to gain insight into how this research works. How do you really conduct literature research? How do you read a text and decide what is important? How do you research sources? How do you select your material? How do you organise your data? You need this knowledge and these skills to reach – via the formulation of a research plan, the adjustment of the research question, and completion of the research – the phase in which you can begin to write. This chapter focuses on the important research phases that precede the writing process, which will be dealt with in the next chapter.

3.1 Five steps towards a definitive research design

As we explained in the previous chapters, doing research and writing an academic publication is a step-by-step process. This is represented in Diagram 2 (page 64]).

step-by-step process

It begins with a provisional research question (1), followed by the exploration of literature (2) in order to position the research in a historical debate. A good question will follow up on earlier debates or throw new light on a neglected theme in the existing historiography. Therefore, to make the question more precise (3), part of the research must already be done. This leads to a *status quaestionis* – the presentation of the historiographical debates on your subject. After this step follows a further exploration and study of the sources (4). Having completed all these steps, you can then write a definitive research plan (5).

Diagram 2: Five steps to a definitive research plan

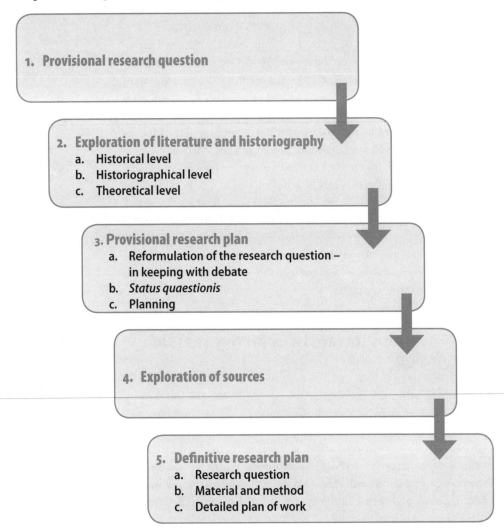

3.1.1 After the provisional research question: Reading strategies on three levels

In Chapter 1, we argued that a historical topic is not yet a historical question. Every research project begins with the translation of the subject into a descriptive, explorative, or explanatory question. This forms the basis for step 2 – the literature research. Exploring the literature is essential not only for giving the research question the necessary precision and for formulating sub-questions but also to place your research in the existing historiography. It is also essential to decide what types of sources are best for you to use or create (as is the case for oral history), and which method(s) can, or must, be applied to analyse these sources. During this step it is always necessary to consult the type of sources that other scholars who have dealt with your topic before have used. Thus, after the provisional research question, every historical research project begins with an exten- *literature research* sive orientation of the existing literature and the state of knowledge in the research field in question. After all, it is necessary to know what has already been done to know what a new contribution could mean. In gen- eral, literature research takes place on three levels – historical, historio- graphical, and theoretical – but not necessarily in that order. You can read the literature on all three levels at the same time by approaching it from different angles. These different levels often overlap.

The first level (2a) involves collecting basic information about your subject: dates of important historical events that are relevant for your *historical level* topic and historical background information about your case such as population figures, biographical data, etc. As can be seen in the diagram, this is not necessarily the first step in your research. More often than not, this historical information will be collected throughout the research in various phases.

The second level of literature research is historiographical research *historiographical* (2b). This means looking at what has been written about the subject *research* previously, what the most important conclusions were, whether a debate has arisen due to these conclusions, and, if so, what the most important positions and developments are in this debate. Are there still significant gaps in our knowledge of the subject? Have questions been raised in that debate that demand more research? At the historiographical level, it is important to look beyond your own specific case study. To return to an earlier example, if you are studying the migration of Huguenots to Amsterdam, it is important not only to look at discussions about this particular case, but also to consult literature about religious refugees in other places in early modern Europe. The snowball method is very use- *snowball method* ful in this phase of your literature research in particular. After all, every good historian relates his work to that of his predecessors. Accordingly, you frequently find references to the most important authors and specific debates that your case relates to. The *status quaestionis* that is part of your provisional research plan (3b) concludes this phase.

The third level of literature research involves setting up the theoreti- *theoretical* cal framework and methodology that you will use for your research (2c). *framework and* Let's say you decide to take a biographical approach. In that case, it is *methodology* important to read studies on the genre of biography in general as well as biographies about your specific subject. If you are interested in the inter- action between long-term developments and particular events in a very specific period, read theoretical works that consider this aspect. During your studies you will become acquainted with all sorts of trends, schools, and theoretical and methodological discussions. With a research project of any size, such as a Bachelor's or a Master's thesis, you will need to find your own position to add force to your arguments.

reading strategies

At each of these three levels of literature research, there are a number of reading strategies that will help you to analyse and process the literature for your research efficiently. An important part of processing literature is assessing the given information. To do this, you must follow three steps. The first is to evaluate the reliability and academic character of the text. The second step is to assess the content of the text (what is the author's argument and how does he present it?). The third step is to formulate your own (academic) opinion on the basis of the text.

academic reliability

For the first step – estimating the academic reliability of the literature – you can first look at a number of extra-textual characteristics. Where does the information come from? Does it come from a well-known publisher or a *peer-reviewed* journal, or is the source of information unknown? Who is the author and what is his or her place in academia? Does the author back the arguments presented with notes? To summarise, this step is about finding out whether the given information can be checked: in other words, what is the source?

analysis

After ensuring the academic level and reliability of the literature, a deeper analysis of the text follows. Apart from collecting historical information, this step is important primarily for obtaining a good idea of the text's argument. At this point, it is very useful to use a step-by-step text analysis in four 'rounds' – a first orientation, a general impression, an intensive reading of specific parts, and an evaluation.

first orientation

To begin with, you want to establish the author's main question or research interest and his or her most important conclusions. For the first orientation, it is sufficient to read the introduction and conclusion – after all, these should contain the research question and main conclusions. When you have gained a first impression of the contents of the publica-

general impression

tion, you should look at the whole text. You can get a rough idea of the structure of the argument by looking at, for example, section headings and the first and last paragraphs of a section,.

When you do this, it is important to look at the structure the author has used – is the text arranged chronologically or thematically? What sort of periodisation has the author used? Only after you have gained a good idea of the general content and are therefore able to follow the argumenta-

intensive reading

tion of the author critically, should you proceed to read the text intensively. As you read, make notes, such as a point-by-point analysis of the argument and the evidence the author uses to support this. Here, it helps to look at the opening and closing sentences of the paragraphs. If the author has organised his or her text well, he or she will often make use of words and references that indicate the structure of the text. Think of words such as 'firstly', 'secondly', 'however', or 'nevertheless'. These help the reader to follow the author's steps. It is important to look at the grounds on which the author makes a statement so that you can compose a well-founded opinion of the argument later. Has the author used only literature, and if so, what? From which sources did the author obtain the information? How were these sources analysed? What has the author not read or seen?

Apart from following the steps described above, it is important to adjust the reading strategy to the type of text. A monograph is read very differently from a contribution to a collection or an article. For example, take note of how a contribution to an edited volume fits within the content of the volume as a whole. It also makes a difference whether an article in a journal stands on its own or whether it is an interim step in a larger research project of the author concerned, and/or whether it is part of a special issue (see also Chapter 2 about types of publication). In general, it is important to ask: what is the author's aim? How is the argument supported? What is the author trying to say, and above all, *why* is he or she trying to say it? *sort of text*

On the basis of the steps described above, you will now be able to form your own opinion of the works you have read and to place them in the historiographical context and debates. In this evaluation of the literature, you must decide whether you found the author's argument convincing: what were the arguments? Did you find the evidence for these arguments convincing? Do you agree with the author's conclusions or do you think that the study has gaps or that the material should be approached in a different manner? For your own research, would you want to start a discussion with this author? *evaluation of the literature*

Now that you have formed your own opinion about the literature you have read, you can place it in a historiographical framework. How has the work been received by other authors?

3.1.2 Back to the research question

As shown in the diagram, after setting up your historiographical framework, it is essential to go back to your research question to re-evaluate it and, if necessary, revise it (3). Is the research question still relevant within the historiographical context, or are there other aspects that are more important to investigate? The most important objective in fitting your research question to the existing historiography is the justification of the relevance of your research. How do you justify your problem definition? What are your most important ideas and concepts? On the basis of the historiography, you can determine reasons to justify your research, such as: *research question evaluation*

- There is a lack of research on a certain subject or part of a subject. In your opinion, there is still (too) little knowledge, and your research can increase our understanding of the subject. Your research contributes something new.
- You are not convinced by the conclusions drawn from existing research because you think the sources that were used are not the right ones or have been used incorrectly. In order to find new and better conclusions, you consider it necessary to analyse the sources with a different method or to expand the current state of research by analysing other sources.
- In your opinion, the theory and/or approach to the topic is wrong, and a different perspective would be more suitable to approach this topic.

Based on the findings of your critical evaluation of the current literature, you are able to formulate a more precise research question. Moreover, it enables you to have a better idea of the sort of sources and methods you intend to use to answer your research question. This certainly does not mean that your literature research is now completed and that you do not need to open another book for the remainder of your research. You will find that during source research, you will constantly be going back to the literature. In addition, it is only during the research that you will discover there is much historical information that is important for your argument, so you must once again turn to the literature. At this stage it can help to *mind map*   make a 'mind map', either on paper or with the help of a computer programme. A mind map is a schematic overview with a provisional organisation of ideas, concepts, structures, and connections based on your main subject. Mind maps are a form of making notes, and if regularly updated they can help the progress of your research.

making notes   The most important advice for all steps of the research process is to make notes – and do not forget to include the place you found the information or ideas that you are going to use. When you read a book, it is easy to be swept along by the flow of the argument and think you can remember it all. However, if later on you need to know the page on which a statement can be found, you will not only waste time looking for it but often will be unable to find it at all.

3.1.3   Research into sources

While working with the literature is reasonably clear, historians are faced with a greater challenge when working with primary sources. After all, *availability*   you are dependent on the *type* of source and its *availability*. Moreover, you *representativeness*   must constantly weigh up how *representative* your sources are. A question you must regularly ask yourself is which types of sources are most suited to answer your main research question and what is the right way to ana-lyse them in order to extract the information needed. After all, (the value of) the information extracted from the sources is never self-evident: it is the historian who gives meaning to the content, puts it into context, and formulates a larger argument on the basis of this information. A histo-rian, therefore, is not someone who simply reproduces the information found in the sources and writes a book based on a series of transcriptions, figures, and other statistical processes, or a series of images or objects.

The first important step in source research is finding the right sources and making a selection of the material available (4). In the previous chap-ter, we gave a number of examples of locations where you can find sourc-es. To find the right sources, it is essential to have a good knowledge of the study subject – *which* sources can you expect, and where can you find these particular sources? When you visit an archive, the most important question to ask yourself is: which organisations, (governmental) insti-tutions, or people had something to do with the subject I am research-ing? This question is important because archival records, unlike digitised texts, are often not searchable by keywords. For example, if you are plan-ning to write something about homosexuality in the Netherlands and you fill in this or a similar term in the search bar of the archive's website, you will only get a limited number of hits. You will only find those records in which the word appears in the archivist's description of the item. It is therefore important that you know where there is a good chance that you will find this information, without the availability of search engines (digital or otherwise) that could lead you straight to it. In this example, in a period when homosexual acts were criminal offences, you could look at the archives of courts of justice. For the fight to remove such acts from the penal code, you could go to those organisations that hold the archives of interest groups and action groups. You can also find out whether there are archives of individuals who are relevant for this research.

Deciding the right research method must relate to your research ques-tion (5a) and the type of source available to answer it (5b). The historian has numerous methods to analyse sources, too many to discuss them all thoroughly here. Roughly, they can be divided into *quantitative* and *quali-tative* research methods. Quantitative research, which makes use of sta-tistical methods for the interpretation of serial data, is carried out chiefly by socio-economic historians. This can be done at a fairly basic level: For example when a researcher wants to chart the pattern of migration to the Republic in the early modern period. A statistical analysis, based on deeds of betrothal, can be made of the number and origin of immigrants in the Republic. Of course, you can make it more complex and advanced by us-ing the statistical methods that are also used in other disciplines, such as calculating correlations or applying a statistical test such as a cross table.

selection of sources

research method and question

quantitative research

qualitative research

Qualitative research does not deal with processing serial data but rather with causal explanations and the analysis of sources at the level of textual (and/or visual or material) content. Here, the historian has a wealth of possibilities. A text can be analysed using a (critical) discourse *combination of* analysis or by *close reading*. In general, historians frequently use a combi-*methods* nation of methods. For instance, statistical research based on serial data into the pattern of the origins of immigrants might be augmented with a qualitative analysis of ego documents of a number of individuals who were migrants. Moreover, the use of just one type of source and approach can cause problems because it gives only a limited view of the situation. In your final work plan (5c), you should give explicit reasons for your choice of material and method.

3.1.4   The importance of source criticism

source criticism

Source criticism is one of the most important aspects a historian must think about when working with sources. In essence, source criticism is nothing more than an explicit reflection on possible distortions in your sources or possible lack of information that can hinder interpretation. To be able to do this properly, it is always important to determine the origin and author of your source, why it was made, why it has been preserved, how unique and how carefully constructed the source is, and other rel-*limitations* evant aspects. It is very important to be conscious of the deficiencies of a *of the source* source and the fact that it is always, by definition, coloured in some way. Unavoidably, the content is a selection based on the choices of the maker. In addition, specific reasons or circumstances have determined why this source was preserved, and others were not. Nevertheless, you should not let this discourage you. It important to be aware of the inadequacies of the source, and then you can get to work on the information that the source *can* give you.

getting the most out A good example of this is working with court records. Much of *of a source* the research done by historians of crime is based on the reports of examinations of the accused and witnesses. Many social historians or political historians make use of these sources as well, for example for research into urbanisation or corruption. As a rule, the researcher working with this type of source is not interested in who was guilty of a crime. The classic 'whodunit' question was central to the actual legal case but is not necessarily interesting to the historian. Moreover, it is impossible to be one hundred percent certain of the answer to that. It is far more interesting to use less charged information that emerges from a court case in research, for example, into social relations or the power relations in the society at the time. Even when the truth about the crime does not emerge in cross examination, the explanations must appear to be credible and consequently reveals a great deal about the social context in which the witnesses or accused operated. *Fiction in the Archives: Pardon Tales and their Tellers in Sixteenth-Century France* by Natalie Zemon Davis and *The Cheese and the Worms: The Cosmos of a Sixteenth Century Miller* by Carlo Ginzburg are two well-known examples of research in which micro and macro history play a role and where the researchers have tried to obtain as much as possible from their sources. Microhistories do not need to be based on a location: in *Werkers van de wereld. Globalisering, arbeid en interculturele ontmoetingen tussen Aziatische en Europese zeelieden in dienst van de VOC, 1600-1800* [*Workers of the world. Globalisation, labour and intercultural encounters between Asiatic and European seamen in the service of the VOC*] by Matthias van Rossum, there is a global perspective on the microcosm of ships.[1]

micro and macro history

3.2   Organising literature and sources

In every step of historical research, it is crucial that the information you have collected and produced is organised in a structured way. When you collect titles for a *status quaestionis*, it is important that you can find them later without searching through a pile of loose notes. Even more important is the organisation of your primary sources, whether they are newspapers, diaries, guild accounts, or photographs. You need to be able to dig up the sources or the information from the sources in an easy and efficient way. The organisation of sources and data is also an important part of the historical method. You must constantly ask yourself: what information can I obtain from this source and how do I organise it to reach a good answer to my research question? What are the typical pitfalls and how can I avoid these? Below are a few pointers.

organise

3.2.1   Making a well-founded reading list

When you have chosen your subject and begin your search for literature, you will notice that you will quickly encounter a mixed bag of titles. Moreover, with the snowball method, you will continue to come across new titles as you read. It is a great temptation to just scribble a note in the margin. In many cases, you will find that later on you only have a vague idea of the title of a book that could be important for your research and that you have forgotten its exact location. It also happens frequently that you note the title but forget the context in which you found it and why you thought it was important for your research. To avoid such confusion

bibliography

keep it up to date

and distraction, it is important to draw up a bibliography and to keep it up to date from the very beginning. This may seem time-consuming at first, but it will unquestionably pay off later on; even in the writing phase, it will save you a lot of work. We shall explain how a good bibliography should be structured in the next chapter. Here, we shall mainly address the logic behind the organisation of your literature during the search process.

Every research consists of various sub-subjects. For example, if you are doing research on migration to Amsterdam in the Golden Age, you will need general information about migration in the early modern period and information about Amsterdam and the Golden Age. Within these subjects, you will probably deal with sub-themes. The most important thing to keep in mind when drawing up a bibliography during the orientation phase of your research is that you organize it along the line of these different sub-themes.

sub-themes

Make a separate bibliography for each sub-theme of your research, possibly with abbreviated titles that refer to the complete list. When you find a new title in the literature, put it into the appropriate theme immediately. If you do this, you automatically record the aspect of your research for which it appeared to be an interesting title. Naturally, it often happens that you will need a book for the whole research: put the abbreviated title under all the sub-themes for which you need it, even if it means that the title is repeated. By organising things accordingly, you will be able to use your notes in a possible follow-up research project. In later research, when you want to examine migration patterns in Ghent in the seventeenth century, for example, you can use your bibliography for Amsterdam again.

Of course, it is possible to make a bibliography with a simple word-processing programme, but this can be very time-consuming. It is advisable to use a specially developed reference programme. There are several on the market, such as EndNote or Zotero. The big advantage of these programmes is that you can easily set up a personal database with bibliographical references. Whichever programme you use, they can all be set up in such a way that the references can be quickly and efficiently searched and sorted via various means such as author, year of publication, tag, or keyword, and you can put the references directly into a text. Moreover, these programmes often offer the option of importing references from a catalogue, such as those of university libraries, into your own reference database, which will save you a lot of typing.

reference programmes

The advantage of computer programmes that organise references is that you have the option of easily arranging your references in a specific reference style. When you have a bibliography for a paper for which you should use the 'De Buck' reference style (see Appendix I), but later you

reference style

want to use the same bibliography for a journal that uses another style, you do not need to rewrite everything yourself; the programme will do that for you. Another advantage is that you have your bibliography at hand and, importantly, the programmes often offer you space for a précis of the work along with the reference, which means that later, when you need the literature again, the content is summed up for you. You can also see straight away why you considered a particular work important.

3.2.2   Making notes

Obviously, during your research you are not just collecting references to the literature but primarily collecting the information they contain. It is advisable to organise this information systematically so that later you can see at a glance which information was important in an article, collection, or book.

systematic organisation of information

There are various ways of doing this, depending on the information you need. Sometimes, it will only be separate bits of (historical) information found in the literature: for example that in Amsterdam in the first half of the Golden Age, forty percent of the population came from outside the Republic. In that case, you immediately record it in the subtheme for which it is important, and consequently you will have the information in the right place. Always make note of the page numbers on which you found the information!

However, academic literature is not a collection of facts from which you can take what you want. In Chapter 2, we discussed the various forms of academic literature and explained that in every case an academic publication contains an argument. It is therefore necessary to not limit yourself to noting the separate pieces of information, because if you do so, you will lose the context of the information, the author's argument. Why did the author include this information in his or her text? Perhaps the information is coloured by the author's argument and other information can be set against it? Diagram 3 is an aid to getting a good idea of this information. Moreover, it helps to organise this information according to subject.

context of the information

As we have already said, it is very important – even if you do not make a full summary – to remember to note the (abbreviated) author and title, including page numbers, when putting down relevant information. If you do not do so at once and accurately, you will need to go to a great deal of trouble later, when you are writing, to give the right literature reference.

Diagram 3: Summary and organisation of the literature

Title	Author, Title, Date of publication
Keywords	Note the most important themes here.
Research question	What was the author's aim?
Hypothesis and/or theoretical framework	The work does not stand on its own. Note the academic tradition and historical framework in which the author places his/her work and which hypotheses in his/her work here emerge from that framework.
Argument	Note the various steps of the research and how the argument is built on these.
Conclusion	What are the author's most important conclusions based on his/her research?
(Historical) information	Take notes of information such as dates / population figures /historical trends and changes.
Sources	What type of sources did the author use in his/her research – diaries, guild accounts, interviews, ego documents? Next to the type of source, note the specific sources the author used, so that later you can check the sources yourself or use them for your research.
Notes	Note down which authors the researcher often refers to. This gives a good overview of the important literature on a subject, and after a time you can see whether these authors refer to each other. Then you can see how much information has been available on the subject up to now and the source of this information.

3.2.3   Keeping a record of sources

The general rules that apply to organising your literature also apply to organising the sources – noting where they come from (so you can find them again) and following a consistent approach. Nevertheless, organising sources is not the same as organising literature. You organise your sources not only for your own administration or to go back to something that is relevant for your research; the information you obtain from sources is often the heart of your research. How you do this is an important part of your methodology. Section 3.3 deals with methodological questions concerning organising your sources. However, first we will give a brief explanation of how you can organise sources to make them suitable for your own use (or setting up your own mini-archive).

It is possible that, as a researcher, you are the first person to work with certain source material and, by doing so, you make it accessible to others. Whatever type of source you use for your research – literature, photographs, guild accounts, diaries, or anything else – it is important that you make – and keep – them accessible to yourself. This is certainly the case when you work with a large corpus of sources. Three things are important and must always be noted: 1) the place where the source is held, 2) the type of source, and 3) the information the source yields.

Do not leap headlong into the information you can use, but think about how the first two points affect the third. However you later organise your sources, whether chronologically, thematically, or alphabetically, always note the name of the holding institution together with the archive, inventory number, and record number. In the case of an interview, note the details and background information of the interviewee, date, place, and time. For an object, note the collection number, place, dating, and context information. Do all this both for notes for qualitative research on primary sources and when collecting (serial) data for quantitative research. Keep a list of the archives and archive items you have consulted, including noting those items in which you have found nothing for your research. That prevents you from asking for the same item twice, because it is easy to forget what lies behind the description in the archive inventory. Again, always record, as clearly as possible, why the source is or is not important. A source that has little to contribute to your research at that moment might be very important another time. Now, at least you know why you rejected this source earlier.

If possible, it is advisable to make a copy or photograph of the source. For example, if your research uses newspaper articles, it is handy to have a scan of the relevant articles. This also applies to when you work with newspaper articles (that have been made accessible online). Many archives allow you to make photographs of archive items you would like to work with, or they can provide you with photocopies. You can often download digitised archive items or make a screenshot of them. Make sure that your own copy always accurately refers to the holding institution of the original (for example, in your document name for it) and that you save it in an organised fashion. Keeping a source (or a copy) yourself has the advantage that it is always at hand, so you are not dependent on the opening times of the library or being able to access the website. After all, the website could be unavailable due to technical problems or you might be working somewhere where you have no access to the internet and consequently cannot get to your source either.

Obviously, not every provider of digitised or online sources offers the opportunity to download the source to your own computer without further ado; sometimes, you must pay for a it. Naturally, it is not possible

finding place of the source

list of archive items consulted

copy of the source

to make a copy of every type of source. Sometimes, it cannot be done because the source is far too big, because it would cost an unreasonable amount of time, or because it is simply too expensive. It also not effective to quickly collect more digital files than you can read or process for your research, so plan your archive research carefully. Often, it takes time to acquire sufficient insight into the structure of a source to develop a system for the clear and useful organisation of information. Then, bearing in mind consistency, you will need to go back to the archive items you first consulted so that you can look at them from the point of view of the system you have developed in the meantime or to check the data.

insight into the structure of the source

As well as ensuring access to your sources, the advantage of setting up your own personalised mini-archive is that you can organise the sources yourself. You can combine data from different sources and corpuses, so that you are no longer dependent on the way in which an archive has arranged its sources, which is probably neither handy nor logical in your case. For instance, an archive could be arranged chronologically, while you may find it more useful to organise things thematically; or an archive has organised items according to name, while you may want to do a comparison by age. A museum organises according to material, but you are looking for objects of various materials made by the same person. A photographic collection might be arranged according to photographer, while you are searching for all the photographs of a particular event.

combining sources

It is important to save your sources and make them as accessible as possible because they reflect the selection you as the researcher have made. To return to the example of the newspaper articles, you often do not use the whole newspaper as a source but select only what is important to you. Accordingly, you will create a new corpus of sources. It is very possible that this selection of sources can be of value to you in research you conduct later, or to others. For this reason alone, it is worth taking the trouble to document everything well. Moreover, the selection often increases the accessibility of the sources for yourself and others.

storing the sources and making them accessible

3.2.4   Practical tips for saving computer files

Lastly, we have a few practical tips for keeping track of both the literature and sources and the analyses you make of them.

working files
- Make sure that you do not save your work in too many places, otherwise you run the risk of accidently working with a file that is not the most recent version.

back-up
- Nonetheless, make sure that you always make a back-up of your work on various carriers. If, for example, your computer crashes, you will still have a recent file of your work; but use these as back-up: do not work on them. Bear in mind the *worst case* scenarios and take precautions.

● Give your files a clear name and also note the date in the title. It can *clear file names* help when writing a paper to save the text as a new file at the end of the day. You could give it a name such as *21-07-2014 Paper*. The next day's work would be *22-07-2014 Paper*. You do not need to keep all the versions; the final version will suffice after you finish your paper or research. This will help you keep a careful eye on your progress and, if necessary, you can retrieve things you had deleted earlier. Moreover, this prevents you from becoming confused about which version to use, and it avoids the loss of data that could occur if you work in the wrong version.

3.3 Organisation is reasoning: Source criticism and the historical method

As well as being part of your administration, organising your sources is also an important part of the historical method. Your research question *historical method* is one of the things that decides the way you search for primary sources and find data that is important for you. Every research question implies that you think along the same lines as the organisation of the archive but *archive organisation* at the same time also 'against' it. To quote an important concept of critical archive research: you go 'along' but also 'against the archival grain'.[2] Grain here refers to the direction of wood fibres (e.g. in paper) or the weave of textiles – this can go across or with the direction. This is meant quite literally – do you follow the archival arrangement and use it for organising the analysis of your sources, or do you go your own way? Another way to put it is: do you read the text 'for what is there' or do you look for implied information?

3.3.1 'Silences' in texts

Source criticism not only concerns the text itself but emphatically also what is not in the text. When you evaluate sources (both textual and visual) critically, it can help to realise that they not only contain 'demonstrable' information but possibly also various kinds of 'silence'. Ann Stoler names *'silence'* three types of silence: what was not written down was completely self-evident so no-one even thought to explain it; something was consciously omitted because it had to be withheld; and lastly, things remain unrecorded because there was a taboo on the subject so that the author could not find the words to describe something that was cloaked in shame or that even literally had no name.[3] Silences are rarely evident and, generally speaking, it is not the first question that enters your head when facing a source. A historian can only search for such silences when he or she has an explicitly formulated research question and a good knowledge of the secondary literature. They can be found in the context of research into slavery, for instance, or the history of homosexuality or persecution due to one's belief, political convictions, or ideology. Although it is not a first approach to studying archives, the example of searching for silences illustrates the direct correspondence between archive research and the historical method.

3.3.2 Periodisation

periodisation

characteristics

Another example of the direct correspondence between archive material and the development of your research findings concerns periodisation. Every historian makes a certain division in time that is helpful in delineating the research and for presenting his or her research findings. We have already mentioned periodisation in connection with the way in which you study the literature. To put it briefly, it has three characteristics: periodisation is a division in time, usually made retrospectively and based on a specific historical question. In the Netherlands, you have perhaps already come across this in secondary school with the periodisation of (Western) history into 'ten ages' beginning with 'the age of hunters and peasants' and ending with 'the age of television and computers'. Other examples include 'the long nineteenth century', a term coined by historian Eric Hobsbawm, which began with the French Revolution and ended with the First World War, followed by the 'short twentieth century' from the First World War to the fall of the Berlin Wall. Indeed, Hobsbawm devised the latter periodisation after 1989. This periodisation is widely accepted by historians, but it is not inconceivable that the concept of the 'short twentieth century' will not be viable in light of the events of the first decade of the twenty-first century. Perhaps even the concept of the 'long nineteenth century' will be abandoned and a new periodisation might be suggested in the historical debate.

3.3.3 Selection

The fact that organizing your sources and your methodology are connected becomes immediately clear when you work with 'big' sources, i.e. sources in which the information is so rich that it is impossible for a researcher to study it in a given time. A good example is the old judicial archives. You must understand that these cover – quite literally – many metres of paper documents and thousands of cases. The criminal sentence records from the early modern period in Leiden consist of 68 volumes, with several hundred cases per volume. In most cases, such sources are not digitised and cannot be digitally searched, so you do not have the option of finding relevant cases by means of search engines. Sometimes you will strike lucky and have registers in which you can find which cases deal with theft, for example, and which with murder. This means you have the option of making a selection of cases that could be relevant for your research. However, even after such a selection, the amount is too *selection* large to sift through. What do you do with such a treasure trove of information? In such cases, you need to take samples. You can do this by taking a number of years that you think are representative. You can also decide to base your selection on other criteria. Whichever criteria you choose, you must be able to justify your method of selection. Why have you chosen these particular years for your sample? It is not always the number of source items that cause a problem but sometimes the nature of the information. Economic historians frequently work with sources such as accounts, taxation records, lists of debts, etc. Such sources often contain an enormous amount of serial and numerical information that you cannot process without aids. In such cases, it will be necessary to put the information into a database yourself so you can do more work with it. Here, too, the organisation of the source, the organisation of your research data, and your choice of delineation and methodology are all connected.

3.3.4 Image analysis

Another example of the way your methodological choices and the nature of the source research are connected, concerns the analysis of photographs. *analysis of* Photographs represent a different relation to the past than written sourc- *photographs* es. They are determined by the situation at the moment the photograph was taken, but equally by what happens to the exposure as a negative and print. You can take many approaches to analysing a photograph. You can make an inventory of what you see to describe the photograph, look for the context in which the photograph was taken, put the aesthetics and intrinsic significance into words, give the photograph's history or what it depicts, or investigate the photographer's involvement in the event.

The institution holding the photograph, where it originates, why it fits in with your research, and whether you have incorporated the photograph into a series are also relevant. You can use Diagram 4 to help you do this systematically. Decide beforehand which aspects of the diagram are most important for your research – the moment the photograph was taken, the possible interaction between the photographer and the situation depicted or the 'biography of the picture', what happened to the print (either unique or a distributed print run). It will be obvious, with such an approach, that the photograph is not just an illustration of what is already known with the help of other sources. The photograph – from passport photos to news photographs, from family albums to governmental archives – contributes to unlocking the past.

Diagram 4: Approaches to the analysis of photographs as historical sources[4]

1. *Descriptive framework*
   - **What do you see?**
   - **Have you any idea what is happening outside the picture, what framework has been chosen for this image?**
   - **What is in the photograph that you do not see (well)?**
2. *Taking the photograph; position and technique of the photographer*
   - **When was the photograph taken?**
   - **Which techniques were available, what technical data can you deduce from the photograph available?**
   - **What implications did the technique have for the actual taking of the photograph (having to keep still for a long time, snapshot, etc.)?**
   - **Who was the photographer and what was his position – professional, amateur, in the service of the police, on a mission, commercial interest, etc.?**
   - **What form of interaction do you suspect there was between the photographer and the subject of the photograph?**
3. *What is represented in the image; consider for example:*
   - **– *Re-enactment* (posing – representing something).**
   - **– A *performance of history* (recording an event or process).**
   - **– A (political, poetic, aesthetic, etc.) statement of the photographer to his public.**
   - **– An aspect of *orality* (as a souvenir of a journey, growing children, etc.).**
4. *The 'biography' of the photograph*
   - **Held in which archive?**
   - **How was it printed?**
   - **Used in what context?**
5. *The photograph as a relational object of writing history*
   - **In which context is it now regarded by the historian?**
   - ***Oral history* as a stimulus to talk about the past.**

3.3.5   Use of oral sources

In the case of *oral history*, the historian has a very different relation to the historical sources. Oral history is based on the stories that people tell of their past, about specific events, their life stories, and their views of the developments of which they have been a part or what they expect the past will mean for the future.

Oral history can address the larger issues or be very private. The re-searcher talks to the people involved and, during the conversation, a new

interview   source concerning the past comes into being. Conversations can be open when the researcher steers the course of the talk as little as possible, but

questionnaire   standard questionnaires are also used – so that they can be compared and quantified – and these are put to various people. There are separate manuals for the method of oral history. In short, it is important to realise that, using oral history, the past acquires its form through talk. A good justification of the method followed is necessary – think of the open conversation, the structured questionnaire, or a mixture of the two, with or without recording instruments (audio, video), with or without supporting visual material to stimulate memories, on 'location', at someone's home, or in formal surroundings such as the university. It is also relevant to make explicit mention of the relation between the researcher and the interviewee – family relations, respondents to an appeal in the newspaper, contact by means of third and fourth parties, etc. Lastly, you must make agreements with the interviewees about how the conversation will be made public and whether the interviewees may see how it has been reproduced by the historian before publication. Will there be a full transcript? To whom will the audio recording be available? And how long will the material be preserved? Nowadays, historians, like anthropologists, usually ask interviewees to sign a consent form in which such agreements are stated.

methodological justification

making public

making agreements

Notes

1   Natalie Zemon Davis, *Fiction in the Archives: Pardon Tales and Their Tellers in Sixteenth-Century France* (Cambridge 1988); Carlo Ginzburg, *De kaas en de wormen. Het wereldbeeld van een zestiende-eeuwse molenaar*, vert. Pietha de Voogd met medewerking van Ruud Ronteltap (Tweede druk; Amsterdam 1989); Matthias van Rossum, *Werkers van de wereld. Globalisering, arbeid en interculturele ontmoetingen tussen Aziatische en Europese zeelieden in dienst van de VOC, 1600-1800* (Hilversum 2014).
2   Ann Laura Stoler, *Along the Archival Grain: Epistemic Anxieties and Colonial Common Sense* (Princeton 2010).
3   Ibidem, 17-18.
4   Based on: Elizabeth Edwards, *Raw Histories. Photographs, Anthropology and Museums* (Oxford/New York, 2001) and Arjun Appadurai (ed.), *The Social Life of Things. Commodities in cultural perspective* (Cambridge, 1986).

This chapter argued that, when finding and organising information, you constantly need to make choices. Where you search, how you read, and how you collect your source material and interpret it all require that you make conscious choices and continually return to your research question. The scheme showing the steps from the provisional research question to the definitive research plan demonstrates this. With each of these steps, the historian will write and so bring together trains of thought, information, and explanations. In the next chapter, the focus will be on the writing process.

4 WRITING HISTORY: NARRATIVE AND ARGUMENT

History is a science in which texts are given much importance. It has already been emphasised that, as a rule, historians present the results of their research as a narrative. Therefore, writing is an important skill for a historian. This chapter deals with writing a historical account. How do you make your own written text from the raw data from literature and sources? How do you build your argument and how do you structure your text? How do you position your text properly in regard to the historical debate? What writing style would be best for you to use? The purpose of this chapter is to give guidelines to help you write a historical argument in which you provide a good historical explanation. After dealing with the organisation of the text (the structure), we will discuss the organisation of the parts of the text (paragraphs), and finally aspects of writing style, tone, and formulation.

4.1   The structure of a historical text

Writing is part of the research and explanation process. Above, we considered the various opinions of what makes a good historical analysis (Chapter 1). The opinions about historical account are relevant to the writing process and can lead to very different sorts of texts. Never- *writing proces* theless, an author does not need to conform to a particular historico-philosophical school of thought to be able to write a good historical account. Certainly, this is not expected of students in the first years of their course. When considering how a historian should write, the question of what makes a good historical analysis is always there in the background. In itself, the text is an individual product, but how- *individual product* ever different they might be, texts are always judged on their merits as historical texts – and for that there are no hard and fast rules. Writing is a skill that varies from individual to individual and that requires the personal creativity of the author. However, guidelines can aid the development of this skill.

After all, the historian does not write just for himself or herself. The aim of an academic text is to communicate information in the clearest possible way. A good text is one that is understood by the reading *reading audience* audience for which it was intended. Elaborate prose filled with figures of speech, the meaning of which is not absolutely clear, misses the mark. For most people, the factors that determine whether a text is comprehensible or not are the same. If the first ten readers are completely unable to understand a text, there is a good chance that the next ten readers will not understand it either. It is therefore not only very possible but also useful to give a number of general rules about writing clearly. *rules of writing*

These rules are not regulations in the sense that an academic text is judged to be unsatisfactory if they are not fully followed. They are a guideline to making a text as comprehensible as possible for the reading audience. The process of writing always starts with the structure of the text – what comes where and in which order?

4.1.1   Introduction

introduction

A historical text of any length starts with a title page and contents. The account itself begins with an introduction that serves to introduce the subject of the research and the research question that the account will answer. It is better not to start the introduction immediately with the research question: the introduction should make the reader gradually acquainted with the subject and introduce the research question. Is the text about a historical person? When did he or she live and how do we know of him or her? Is the subject a particular period or event? Which period is it or where and when did the event happen? What is characteristic of the period or event? The subject can also have a more abstract nature. If the account deals with increasing individualism in Western Europe since the twelfth century, it is important to define what is meant precisely by 'individualism' in this case. This is a concept that could refer to a whole range of ideas and practices. To avoid a lack of clarity, the author should carefully explain in the introduction which definition is the basis of the research.

introduction of the subject

The research question arises from the subject and therefore should follow the introduction of the subject. When the question is announced, the reader should be acquainted with the significance and background of all the concepts, historical persons, and ideas central to the research question. It must be made clear why the question is relevant for an academic study. As we explained earlier, the research question forms a 'bridge' or 'lever' which determines what contribution a particular research project (and therefore the research report) will make to a debate or to existing insights (see also Chapter 1). The relevance of the question to the research and what the historical account will contribute to existing academic knowledge must be clear from the introduction. In fact, the question must be justified.

relevance

research method

After this part of the introduction, it is important to explain how the research was carried out and to discuss the research method and, if relevant, the theories you used. This is usually done in the introduction, but you could alternatively put more extensive considerations of theory and methodology in a separate chapter.

Whether you choose to include a theoretical chapter in the paper or use the introduction to discuss it, the basic structure of the text does not change. Theoretical considerations in the introduction always follow the introduction of the subject, the research question and justification. A

separate theoretical and methodological chapter always follows the introduction but comes before the other substantive chapters.

Lastly, it is useful to give a brief outline of the structure of the text   *structure*
or argument in the introduction, so the reader knows what to expect.
When you do that, you can refer to the steps of the argument or text, but
you could also summarise each chapter in one or two sentences in the
order in which they appear. Some authors find this unnecessary — after
all, it is clear during the reading of the text which chapters are included.
Yet, a brief note of what is to come can be helpful. Such a brief sketch
gives the reader an overview and a handhold whilst reading and makes
the general lines of the argument apparent. By doing so, you allow the
reader to follow the argument more easily. Readers who are interested
in only part of the text can estimate the function of each chapter in the
account.

A good introduction therefore consists of: 1) an introduction to the   *elements of a good*
subject, 2) the research question, 3) the justification of the question, 4)   *introduction*
a presentation of the theory and method, and 5) an overview of the following chapters. Writing the introduction is not the first time you will
consider the content of your account. The process of thinking of a subject
and question begins when you set up the research (see Chapter 1).

Many historians only start the introduction when they have complet-   *order of work*
ed all the chapters. After all, during the research, it might be necessary
to adapt the research question, which could mean that the final form of
the research question is known only in a later phase. However, it can be
useful to write the introduction first, as this provisional introduction can
function as a sort of guide when writing the other chapters. The introduction determines what you will address in each chapter and therefore
leads the text and the separate chapters in a particular direction. If you
write the introduction before you begin writing the chapters, you avoid
the risk of losing the cohesion between the various chapters.

4.1.2 Introduction and preface

As well as an introduction, many studies include a preface. This can be an
acknowledgement that serves chiefly to thank people or institutions who
have helped the author during the research. Accordingly, expressions of   *acknowledgements*
thanks do not belong in the introduction. An author can also use a pref-
ace to share thoughts with the reader that are only indirectly connected
to the subject of the account. For instance, in a book about Charlemagne,
the historian might include remarks about the study of mediaeval history
in the preface. A preface can almost always be omitted in a paper, while it
is more usual to thank those who have helped reading versions and cor-
rections in the preface of a Bachelor's or Master's thesis.

To decide whether information belongs in a preface or in the introduc-tion, the general rule is that everything said in a preface can be omitted without the risk of the reader being unable to understand the main text. By contrast, everything in the introduction is essential if the reader is to follow the argument.

4.1.3   The argument

chapters and sections The introduction is followed by the individual chapters that as a whole form the argument of the book. They present the reader with the results of the historical research. The research results should always be presented to the reader in an organised fashion. The information that belongs to-gether is grouped in sections and chapters so that the argument is clear, enabling the reader to know which role each statement has in the broader argument. In essence, the argument can be organised in two ways – dia-chronic and synchronic.

diachronic organisation Diachronic means 'through time': when an argument is structured dia-chronically, a development is described as it takes place over time. In this case, the order of the chapters is chronological: events that took place ear-lier are described in the first chapters, while later events are dealt with in later chapters. The author decides where the boundaries between periods lie, as given in the separate chapters; the past itself dictates no absolute boundaries between periods, and the periodisation is part of the histo-rian's personal analysis. The choice of a particular chronological periodi-sation must be justified by explaining, either at the beginning or end of each chapter, why the particular period of time examined in that chapter must be regarded as a separate period in light of the account's subject.

division into periods of time In Chapter 3, we took a brief look at periodisation: the division into segments of time made in retrospect from the point of view of a par-ticular research question. Historians often have different opinions on the best periodisation. For example, in a study of the Cold War, one historian may claim that the launch of the Sputnik in 1957 to the moon landing in 1969 should be seen as a period. Another may choose the break between China and the Soviet Union in 1961 and Nixon's visit to the Chinese People's Republic in 1972 as the beginning and end of a *integrative principle* period. In the case of the first periodisation, the integrative principle is the period of the space race; in the case of the second, it is China's shift in political alliances. Because the past does not have a structure of itself, one choice is not better than the other. It is up to the reader to judge whether the chosen periodisation is successful in explaining the past and making it comprehensible.

When you structure a diachronic text, you must consider the themes that determine how the historical narrative is told. This choice decides how the periods handled are divided and which historical facts are reported and which are omitted. Only rarely does a historian divide his narrative in such a way that each chapter deals with a period of exactly the same length of time. A chapter discussing a period of three years and another that considers developments over ten years can go together perfectly well. Nor does it mean that a chapter dealing with the events of a shorter period needs to be shorter than a chapter dealing with a longer period. There is no hard and fast rule regarding the relationship between a historical account and the time as recorded by the calendar: some periods simply require more explanation to clarify or describe certain developments. However, you must remember to always refer to specific dates.

Many historical studies use a different organisation principle, i.e. a synchronistic arrangement. Synchrony means 'at the same time'. In that case, the historian does not describe changes over time but instead looks at a particular period in the past and examines various aspects of this period or historical phenomenon. *synchronistic organisation*

For instance, the first chapter deals with political relations in the given period, the second with religion and culture, and the third with the economy. The chapters could also concentrate on various causes for a certain historical phenomenon. Here, too, the choice of how the divisions are made is subjective. In reality, politics, culture, and the economy are always connected. Various causes could be closely related to each other in the past, or various actors might have had their own roles but not necessarily independent of each other. The thematic division is created by the historian to make the past clearer or to phrase the argument better.

An argument with a primarily synchronistic structure can be divided in many ways. In addition to a *thematic* scheme, you can use a *geographic* set-up whereby you analyse the historical situation in various places. There is also the *evaluation* scheme in which you introduce a particular historical question and use each chapter to address a different historical viewpoint of the problem. In the various chapters, it is important to concentrate on the sub-questions into which the main research question is divided. This ensures that you do not discuss any analyses that are not relevant to answering the main question. You must also bear in mind that even a synchronic account refers to general diachronic historical knowledge. An academic study never stands on its own but is part of a broad debate. In the discipline of history, much of this debate concerns how to explain changes over time. In essence, history is a diachronic science. Synchronic studies contribute to the knowledge of a specific moment and period in history that can be incorporated into a diachronic analysis later on. In synchronic studies, you make references that enable *geographic division* *evaluation division dates* scholars to link the work to diachronic knowledge. The most obvious example is noting dates. Even a synchronic study is set in time through the use of dates. By this means, an informed reader will know the relationship between the synchronic study and general diachronic knowledge of the past.

mixed forms No historical study is purely diachronic or synchronic. In every historical text, the two forms are used together, but it is important to use one form or the other as a guideline when you structure your argument. It will cause confusion if some chapters have a diachronic relation with each other while others are based on synchronic organisation.

4.1.4   The conclusion

Every academic text ends with a conclusion in which the research question is revisited and answered. The *Van Dale* dictionary defines 'conclusion' as inference or outcome. The conclusion is the moment in the account in which the research question is answered, either positively or negatively. This suggests that, in the argument, a number of statements are made from which, in the conclusion, new knowledge arises by means of deduction. For example, if the first chapter demonstrates that if statement A is true, statement B is also true, and in chapter two it is revealed that statement A is indeed true, then the conclusion must be that statement B is true. This form of logic is characteristic of the exact sciences.

In the humanities, of which history is one discipline, this form of logic is far less usual. The aim of historical research is the description and explanation of changes over time. For instance, the historian wants to know how the struggle for political hegemony over Central Asia between the Russian Empire and Great Britain developed in the period between 1813 and 1907. This question would probably be answered by a diachronically structured study in which each chapter deals with a certain period and the term 'Central Asia' increasingly acquires a greater degree of specification. Accordingly, the research question is gradually worked out in the process of the argument. It is difficult to imagine how that could lead to a conclusion according to the logical reasoning system given above. That is

summary why, in a historical study, the conclusion often has the form of a summary. The reader is led briefly through all the chapters by which the research question is answered.

synthesis However, the conclusion is more than a simple summary: it forms a synthesis that brings together all the new elements in the argument in a systematic answer to the main question. The summary of the argument in the conclusion is part of this synthesis. Moreover, the conclusion is the

implications part where the scholar presents and clarifies the implications of the research results. The main question of a research project relates to a debate and the existing literature: so what do the findings and conclusions of the research mean for broader historical insights and debates? In the conclusion, the historian considers the new results and explicitly states their implications. Sometimes these considerations are new historical insights, but often they are new historical questions or recommendations for new research.

4.2   Guidelines for the division of paragraphs and sections

So far, we have dealt with the general structure of a historical account. Now we should drop down to the level of the structure of an argument. At this level, the paragraph is the smallest unit, with sections or subheadings to support the argument's progress.

4.2.1   One paragraph per point or one message per paragraph

Texts are divided into paragraphs. They do not function solely to make the text look clearer: they serve primarily to give structure to the argument. A paragraph cannot be placed in the text arbitrarily. The start of a new paragraph marks the start of a new part of the argument. Strictly speaking, not every paragraph has its own (partial) subject. Subsequent paragraphs can have the same subject: they can be separated from each other because they say something different about that subject. In a text, therefore, various paragraphs can share a subject, but each has its own message or makes its own point. The difference between the two is that a subject can be summarised in a word or two, while a point or message can only be expressed in a sentence. If someone were to put the subject of all the paragraphs in one or two words and set them down in a list, it is highly likely that the list would contain the same word several times. However, if the message of each paragraph is summarised in a sentence, the list should show that each sentence is clearly different from all the others.

paragraphs

A paragraph is thus integrated by the specific point that the author wants to make. It is important to keep this in mind when writing a paragraph. Everything you want to say about such a point or message in your text must be brought together in this paragraph. If there are other sentences in your argument that contribute to a point you made in an earlier paragraph, get rid of the repetition or put them in the earlier paragraph. An exception to this is when you refer back to an earlier statement so that you can jog the reader's memory at a later stage in the argument. You do not need to go back to the original paragraph when making a summary either – as in the conclusion – when you deal with the message of a specific paragraph. When you have this sort of repetition, try to vary your word usage and sentence structure and do not repeat a paragraph literally in a later summary or conclusion. Other than that, abide by the rule of one paragraph *one message per* per point and one message per paragraph. Sometimes, this means combin- *paragraph* ing two paragraphs; after writing a first version, you can check the function of each paragraph. Decide which sentence can summarise each paragraph, and if two seem to be very similar, perhaps they are better combined. In most cases, a great deal of text can be scrapped from these double paragraphs. Sometimes it is better to just eliminate one of the two paragraphs completely.

A paragraph should be a complete unit. The point that is introduced at the beginning should be fully made before you start the next paragraph. It is therefore not advisable to begin a paragraph with 'after all' or 'moreover'. Such words indicate that something – an explanation or elaboration – in the sentence adds to what has been stated in the previous sentence and therefore the sentences are part of the same point and should not be spread over more than one paragraph.

main sentence A paragraph can be built up in two ways. First, the main sentence that expresses the central point of the paragraph can be put at the beginning. In the following sentences, the central point of the paragraph should be clarified and elaborated. A second option is to work towards the main sentence gradually. In this case, the main sentence is not placed at the beginning but halfway through or at the end of the paragraph. The first sentences lead in increments to the main message of the paragraph. The central sentence follows on from the previous sentences and therefore does not need further clarification.

not too long A paragraph must not be too long. The previous paragraph consists of 102 words. Four hundred words is a very substantial paragraph. If you feel that you need so many words, the paragraph can often be split in two because two or more points are being made. Even when you are convinced that a paragraph of a thousand words is making only one point, it is possible to split it up. The points that you make are not dictated by the subject of your argument: as the author, you have the freedom to express your argument in various ways, so it is up to you to decide whether to divide a point into two sub-points. This is to be preferred because it is easier for the reader to follow the argument in such cases.

splitting paragraphs In many cases, it will not be necessary to divide a paragraph that is too long. Very often, it can be shortened by removing double or unnecessary sentences. Do not be reticent in doing so. Just as there should not be any double paragraphs in a section, avoid saying the same thing twice in a paragraph. Two beautifully crafted sentences that express the same message still make a badly flowing paragraph. Even sentences that do not have an equivalent with the same meaning in a paragraph, must always be examined critically. Bear in mind which point you are making in the paragraph, then check whether each sentence contributes to bringing across that point. If the point of the paragraph is not damaged by scrapping the sentence, it is better to just remove it immediately. It can be annoying to remove beautiful sentences, but remember that the quality and beauty of a text is not determined at the level of the individual sentence.

To make it easier to delete sentences, you can open a second text file. You can save beautifully expressed sentences that do not fit into in your text, at least in the first instance, in this file. If you want to use them later, you can find them easily, changing the writer's motto 'kill your darlings' to the less drastic 'ban your darlings'.   *'kill your darlings'*

4.2.2   Examples of organising principles at paragraph level

To conclude this explanation of dividing a text into paragraphs, we shall give a few examples in which various organisation principles are used. There should be a new paragraph when the account takes a new turn in   *turns*
a chronological structured narrative or when a new phase begins in the history in question. This organisation and phasing is determined by the historian him- or herself, depending on which facet he/she would like to emphasise. We have an example of such a division below.

> In the middle of the sixth century BCE, the emergent Persian Empire reached the west coast of Asia Minor. In 547, the Persian king Cyrus (559-530) conquered Lydia and thereby gained sovereignty over the Greek cities on the west coast of Asia Minor that the Lydians had conquered shortly before. In most of these Greek cities, the Persians installed local aristocrats favourable to them as tyrants. They governed the cities under the supervision of the Persian satraps.
>
> In 499 BCE, the Greeks of Asia Minor tried to rid themselves of their tyrants and free themselves from Persian rule. Their attempt failed. In 495-494, the Persians put down this revolt by victories both on land and sea. Shortly after, in 492, the Persian king Darius I (522-486) organised a penal expedition against Athens which had helped the rebels with a small fleet. The Persians travelled by sea, landing at Marathon in Attica, but were defeated by the Athenian hoplites under the leadership of Miltiades (490 BCE). This battle brought Athens renown throughout the Greek world. Sparta stayed out of the Ionic revolt and the fighting of 490, although it had favoured Persia for half a century and at that time was the strongest military power in Greece.

> Ten years later (480), Darius' successor Xerxes once again turned to the matter. He had come to the conclusion that his sovereignty of Asia Minor would only be safe if he could conquer the free Greeks in their homeland and left with a large army and fleet for Greece...
>
> Taken from: L. de Blois & R.J. van der Spek, *Een kennismaking met de Oude Wereld [An introduction to the Ancient World]* (Sixth, revised edition; Bussum 2006) 95-96. Our translation.

In the first paragraph, the reader learns how the Persians gained power in western Asia Minor. All the sentences describe the acquisition and consolidation of this power. The following paragraph begins with the Greek revolt against Persian rule: this is a turn of events in the narrative and therefore starts a new paragraph. Only three sentences deal with this revolt, but clearly the authors regard this event as the beginning of a period in which there were hostilities between Persians and Greeks. The authors organise the past in such a way that the events between 499 and 490 BCE are seen as part of the same historical trend (namely the Greco-Persian hostilities), so the events that took place over a period of ten years can be discussed in the same paragraph.

alternative division   This paragraph division could have been different. If the authors had wanted to write a book that covered a shorter period but gave more detail about what happened in this period, the paragraph division would undoubtedly have been different. The revolt of 499 BCE, the defeat of this revolt in 495-494, and the penal expedition of Darius I in 492 could all have been described in separate paragraphs.

Or they could have chosen to write about a still longer period in still less detail. In that case, it is probable that the Greco-Persian quarrels of 499 BCE would be described in the same paragraph as Darius I's expedition of 490, which, in the text cited above, was seen as a new turn of events and thus the beginning of a new paragraph. The division of the paragraphs is not determined by the past but by what the historian has to say about it.

indication of date   With a chronologically structured text, it should always be clear to the reader which moment in time a specific part of the text is discussing. In the example above, the authors begin each new paragraph by indicating the date. Whenever you begin a new paragraph because a new phase in the historical narrative has begun, you cannot omit giving the date.

summary   The division of the text into paragraphs does not follow only chronological principles. For instance, new paragraphs can be made with a summary. This can be a summary of various arguments to support the author's opinion or a summary of various characteristics of a historical phenomenon, as is the case in the next example:

The Frankish kingdom of the Merovingians – the name of the royal house, taken from the legendary ancestor Merovech – differed from other Germanic kingdoms in the west of the former Roman Empire in three respects. Firstly, the Franks had not migrated, as had many Germanic tribes, but had remained along the Rhine and Meuse and had spread their power out from there. (...)

Secondly, the Franks did not expand only to the south, taking increasingly larger parts of Gaul, but also to the east, which had never been under Roman rule. As well as Burgundy and Provence, Clovis' son annexed Bavaria and Thuringia. In the areas that had never been Romanised, the Franks were not barbarians but the people who brought Roman civilisation and Christianity.

Thirdly, Clovis was the first Germanic king to convert to Catholicism. Before his baptism in 496 or a little later in the cathedral of Reims, all Germanic rulers were heathen or Arian. Therefore, between the conquerors and the Romanised population – largely Catholic in the towns, mostly heathen in the countryside – there remained a religious gulf. (...)

Taken from: Istvan Bejczy, *Een kennismaking met de middeleeuwse wereld* *[Getting to know the mediaeval world]* (Second, revised edition; Bussum 2004) 21-23. Our translation.

In this example, the author makes an analysis in which a phenomenon (the difference between the Merovingians and other Germanic kingdoms) is demonstrated by three separate points. It is important that these steps in the author's reasoning can be followed as carefully as possible so that the reader can evaluate the analysis properly. For this reason, the author uses an explicit summing up (the terms firstly, secondly, and thirdly) and starts a new paragraph for each characteristic mentioned. The structure of the paragraphs should reflect the structure the author is using to think about the past, as is the case here.

Not all paragraphs are equally important for the general line of the argument. Sometimes, an example is given in a paragraph with a statement from a previous paragraph. That is case in the following passage:

clarification and support

Making a sharp caesura between 'civilised' and not (yet) 'civilised' peoples deprives us of the possibility of using 'developed' or 'civilisation' as an umbrella term that, in principle, is applicable to the socio-cultural and socio-psychological development of people in every society. It can be argued against this that we already have such a term, namely 'culture'. A disadvantage of this last term is the strongly static implications of the word: it indicates accomplishments and not the process by which these accomplishments were achieved or changed.

> The American anthropologist Ruth Benedict in her widely read book
> *Patterns of Culture* gave a splendid description of three different cultures
> and of the formative influence that these cultures had upon the indivi-
> duals who grew up in them. She consciously ignored the question of
> how these three cultures came into being. In this respect, the motto that
> she gave her book speaks volumes; she cites a Digger Indian who said,
> 'In the beginning, God gave each people a beaker of clay and from that
> they drunk their life.'
>
> Taken from: J. Goudsblom, *Vuur en beschaving* [*Fire and Civilisation*]
> (Third edition; Amsterdam 2001) 19. Our translation.

The reference to Ruth Benedict's book is an example of the static use of
the term 'culture' as it is mentioned in the last sentence of the first paragraph. This example is certainly relevant to the passage because the author is showing that his statement about the use of the term 'culture' has a
solid foundation. A general statement from the first paragraph is clarified
and supported by referring to a concrete instance. For historians, it is important to constantly support general statements with concrete evidence.

essential
paragraphs   The second paragraph of the example above is not absolutely essential
to the argument. Even without this example, the reader knows the author's view on the use of the term 'culture'. It is useful to be aware of the
difference between *essential* paragraphs, in which the main argument is
supporting   revealed step by step, and *supporting* paragraphs that clarify and support
paragraph   the argument with concrete references. The balance between these two
types of paragraphs has to be just right. Without examples and illustrations, a historical account is a purely theoretical exercise that does not
seem to be grounded in actual historical research. Of course, the reader
must not be overwhelmed by a deluge of historical facts that are of only
secondary importance to the argument.

4.2.3   Section, subsection, subheadings

In addition to paragraphs, section titles and subsection titles (or subheadings) can help to structure the text. In newspapers and magazines,
subheadings serve chiefly as a visual means to give the text a clearer appearance. In academic texts, their primary function is to add to the structure of the argument. In articles, which by definition are of limited length,
subheadings are usually sufficient. In the case of larger works, under the
chapter headings the text is usually divided into sections and subsections,
with their titles organising the text at the level between chapters and
paragraphs.

In historical accounts written in a literary tradition, it is not common to number sections, subsections, or subheadings. Because this guide is a *numbering* textbook, we have done so here. However, in historical works, the sub-heading usually differs from the body text as regards typography (italic, *typographic* bold, underlined, or a different font size). When preceded by a blank line, *differentiation* the subheading creates a breathing space and heralds a new direction in the argument. The heading can be one or two keywords and possibly a short sentence or a question, but never an exclamation. It indicates the subject of the next part of the text. The subheading is not part of the body text. A question or statement made in the subheading should therefore be repeated in the body text. A balanced spread of subtitles should be made within a chapter, and the length of the various parts of a chapter should not be too varied. Just as main titles first draw the reader's attention to a work, the subtitles within a chapter are the first things that catch the reader's eye and invite further reading.

A paragraph with a subject that emphatically deviates from the sub- *line of argument* heading is clearly in the wrong place in the argument. Similar paragraphs should be placed close to each other under the same heading. The use of subheadings not only organises the text for the reader but can also help the author to decide the right place for various passages and paragraphs.

4.3 Argument and debate

In the academic world, the aim is to continually expand and renew exist- ing knowledge. This occurs by means of debate. This debate involves all *debate* the academic publications within a particular field. An academic account is therefore, by definition, written as part of a debate. By sharing research results and findings in publications, historians can build on the work of others, relieving them from the necessity of starting from scratch. New historical interpretations of known historical facts are also presented in this way. Depending on whether the arguments are convincing or not, they can be accepted or rejected by other historians. To conduct the de-bate with precision, it is important that it is always clear whose voice is being heard in a historical account. It must be clear to everyone who wants to take part in the debate whose ideas they are. Is an observation that of the author him or herself, or is he or she quoting someone else?

4.3.1 The voice of the author in the historical account

In this context, it is necessary to realise that the author of an academic text is never 'absent'. The past itself does not exist in narrative form, so there can be no question of a narrative that coincides exactly with an *argumentation* objective past. Consequently, writing a historical account is a form of argumentation. When the historian describes a particular period, it is not a 'neutral' view of the past but a specific vision. In an academic account, the author's voice is present in every description. The reader of a novel can let himself or herself be swept away into the world of the book, and the person who wrote those words can be forgotten. The reader of an academic text does as well to bear in mind who is speaking to him in this text. The academic must be aware that there are always other ways of understanding the past and should continually judge how these ways – in his or her opinion – relate to the views he/she is becoming acquainted with while reading the account.

author's presence In the accepted style of writing a historical account, the author's presence is not immediately apparent. It is not necessary to say that every statement is an idea of the author in question. If a historian began each sentence with 'I argue that...' or 'I suggest that this period should be regarded as...', the text would be unreadable. As a rule, the historian uses a style which makes it seem as if the reader is looking directly at the past. Thus, although the author of an academic text is present in every description, that presence is often implicit.

implicit presence The implicit nature of the author's presence also means that an academic text – whether it is a paper, a Master's thesis, or an article – never looks like a work report. The narrative of the past must be read as the voice of the author, but the reader must not be bothered by remarks about how the author came to write this text. It means that there should not be any sentences like 'I have decided to shorten this chapter because I could not find sufficient source material'. The completed text is the means by which the author takes part in the historical debate. The reader judges the final form of the historical account and not the process by which the account has come into being.

In the introduction to a book, the author sometimes tells readers that he originally had another idea about what he or she was going to write, but with further insight decided on a different direction. In such cases, the introduction must be read as separate from the central argument. Remarks about how the text came about should not be found in the argument itself.

explicit presence At some points in the text, the implicit presence of the author is briefly abandoned and the author will change to an emphatic form of argumentation. In these cases, you can find such statements as 'Others will claim (...) but I do not accept this and argue that...' This concerns the most hotly contested aspects of the academic debate. Some statements about the past are so contentious that historians choose to take the debate explicitly into the text and thereby make their arguments as emphatic as possible. The explicit debate is found more often in articles

than in books and is rarely used throughout the text. In many historical accounts, it does not appear at all and the author's presence remains
implicit throughout the text.

Because writing a historical account is a form of argumentation, the
historian should be conscious of his or her tone. The author's opinion *tone*
of his or her subject should not be mentioned to the reader in a veiled
way but must be communicated explicitly. The arguments of an academic
text must be clear so that the text can be placed in the broader debate. If
the author seems to give an implicit judgement by means of a suggestive
writing style, this is likely to be perceived as annoying and disturbing. The
reader must be able to evaluate the text without having to interpret what
is implied between the lines.

The author him- or herself is not always aware of the implicit judge-
ments that can creep into an account due to the choice of style. A sug- *suggestive tone*
gestive tone is the result of the use of figures of speech and adjectives. A
text without any figures of speech or adjectives can be dry and boring, so
even historians use them. When a historian uses them, he or she must
consider other factors than the novelist. In literary writing, information
is given that is created within the story itself. The author of a novel uses
figures of speech and adjectives to create a world that is born of the text.
By contrast, the academic writes about a world that exists (or existed)
outside the text, which means that figures of speech have a different function than in a literary text.

Figures of speech and adjectives in historical texts have a supportive *figures of speech*
function: they serve the purpose of creating an understanding of the past. *and adjectives*
Accordingly, the historian must constantly ask two questions. First, does
the figure of speech or adjective help to make my explanation of the past
comprehensible to the reader? Second, is the image evoked by the figure
of speech or adjective sufficiently borne out by the results of historical
research? The historian must not qualify a particular historical trend or
event with such adjectives as 'horrific', 'undesirable', or 'splendid' if no arguments are given that would justify such a qualification. Without support,
these kinds of descriptions are suggestive and therefore have no place in
an academic account.

4.3.2 The voice of others in the historical account

Historians work together in the debate to form historical knowledge.
Every historical text refers to the work of others. If an author mentions *work of others*
an idea of another historian, the work of that other historian should be
mentioned in the footnotes.

Very general historical knowledge does not demand footnotes. For instance, if you write that the storming of the Bastille took place in 1789,

you do not need to mention the textbook in which you first came across that fact. There must always be a footnote for a statement that is derived from research or analyses that are specific to a certain work, a certain author, or a particular school of historical thought. The historian Simon Hart worked out that in 1600, forty percent of the population of Amsterdam consisted of foreign immigrants.[1] This historical fact has a very specific origin in Hart's research. If another author wants to mention that fact, he or she must refer to the research that produced this fact. Mentioning the interpretation of facts that can be specifically attributed to a certain author must also be accompanied by a footnote.

footnote   Footnotes are not placed randomly: they always follow the sentence in which the statement is made to which the footnote refers, i.e. directly after the last character ending the sentence (see rules for notes in Appendix I). If the reference concerns the whole passage, then the footnote comes at the end of the paragraph. In exceptional circumstances, a footnote will refer not to a whole sentence or passage but to a single word. In this case, the footnote is placed immediately after the word. If this word is at the end of a sentence, the footnote follows the word directly but before the full stop at the end of the sentence. When arranged this way, it is clear that the reference is made to that last word only and not the whole of the sentence. Remember that this reference must apply *only* to the specific word next to which it is placed, for example, to clarify a particular historical or little-known word. Such references are rare in historic accounts.

4.3.3   Original work and plagiarism

The historian's craft demands that you immerse yourself in the opinions and ideas of others and that you apply them in your argument or refute them. When you do so, it is important that you are very clear about what your own contribution is and what is that of another – this is what is meant *reference*   when we speak of 'original work'. A reference shows that you are conversant not only with certain relevant literature but also with where particular information can be found. References are made for the readers so that they can check those particular findings or use the references themselves and build on your research. It is just as important that when you place the reference you make it clear that the idea did not originate with you but that you borrowed knowledge or insights from another person. It is part of the historiographical debate mentioned above.

Careful annotation, therefore, is fundamental to the historian's discipline. Using the insights or knowledge of others without references *plagiarism*   means you are guilty of plagiarism. When we consider plagiarism, we first of all think of literally taking sentences from the texts of others (cut and paste) and presenting them as if you had written them yourself. That is, of course, absolutely forbidden; but 'theft' of ideas also falls under the heading of plagiarism, as does the literal translation of texts, for example from English to Dutch, without reference to the original English version. Be transparent, position yourself, and ensure that it is clear where your ideas come from. All academic institutions, both in the Netherlands and abroad, have strict guidelines concerning plagiarism.

4.3.4   Examples of one's own argument and references to others

The historian can have various relations with the works to which he or she refers. If the idea of another historian is integrated into the account, so that if the footnote were to be omitted it would no longer be possible to detect the origin of the idea, the author endorses the idea of his colleague. *borrowing*
The argumentation of the historian referred to is incorporated into the ar- *argumentation*
gument of the text. An example of this is a description from a book by J.R. McNeill and William H. McNeill about a shift in power that took place in both America and Asia in the first millennium of the common era.[2]

> Priests eventually ceded primacy to warriors, for straightforward rea-
> sons. For when priestly management succeeded in creating substantial
> surpluses, organized robber became a feasible way of life. This opened
> a niche for professional fighting men to protect communities from
> plunderers by monopolizing organized violence in return for negotia-
> ted protection payments. Specialized weaponry, discipline, and training
> gave such warriors combat superiority over most raiders and robbers,
> allowing both farmers and warriors to benefit from predictable rents and
> taxes as opposed to the ruinous costs of plunder. Accordingly, profes-
> sional warriors could and did compel established priestly elites to accept
> subordination or some form of alliance.[1]

In footnote 1 at the end of this paragraph, it states: *borrowing*

> [1] These patterns are persuasively set forth in Johan Goudsblom, Eric
> Jones, and Stephen Mennell, *The Course of Human History: Economic
> Growth, Social Process and Civilization* (Armonk, NY 1996) 31-62.

McNeill and McNeill (father and son) apparently gained their knowledge of the shifting power relations between priests and soldiers in large
part from the book by Goudsblom, Jones, and Mennell, which is duly
noted in the footnote. Although the McNeills refer to their colleagues
to whom they are indebted, it does not mean that this view of the past is
to be attributed only to Goudsblom et al. In the passage cited above, the

McNeills have made that idea a part of their own narrative about the past and as a consequence, the idea is also part of the McNeills' argumentation of how the past can be understood.

The ideas of historians with whom you disagree cannot be mentioned without explicitly rejecting them. By simply referring to an author in a footnote it is not clear if you agree with his/her statements or not. If the historian mentions the ideas of other researchers in his or her account without clearly rejecting them, he or she is deemed to be in agreement with them.

Sometimes in a historical account, the academic debate is considered directly. Here, the historian whose ideas are discussed is named in the *explicit attribution* body text. By explicitly attributing these ideas to another historian, in contrast to the case we discussed above, they are *not* integrated into the author's argument. It is essential, when doing this, to remember whose views are given in the text, as in the following example.

> According to Ankersmit, an appeal to historical facts is not thereby justified, because although the historian constructs the cohesion *with the help of* the facts, they are in no way to be traced back to the facts. At most, the facts are the building blocks of the narrative, but which edifice is built with them, the historian, as architect of the narrative, decides himself. Therefore, the narrative is more than the sum of the facts mentioned in it, just as a building is more than the sum of its building materials.
>
> Taken from: Chris Lorenz, *De constructie van het verleden. Een inleiding in de theorie van de geschiedenis* [*The construction of the past. An introduction to historical theory*] (eighth edition; Amsterdam 2006) 109. Our translation.

In this paragraph, Chris Lorenz discusses an idea of his fellow philosopher of history Frank Ankersmit. The statements about the role of facts in the historical narrative are therefore not a reflection of Lorenz's historico-philosophical vision; Lorenz is simply explaining Ankersmit's view. The passage above must actually be read thus:

> According to Ankersmit, an appeal to historical facts is not thereby justified, because although the historian constructs the cohesion *with the help of* the facts, they are in no way to be traced back to the facts. **According to Ankersmit**, at most, the facts are the building blocks of the narrative, but which edifice is built with them, the historian, as architect of the narrative, decides himself. **According to Ankersmit**, therefore, the narrative is more than the sum of the facts mentioned in it, just as a building is more than the sum of its building materials.

Stylistically speaking, it is not very pleasant reading to encounter the phrase 'according to Ankersmit' three times within three sentences. Lorenz mentions it only at the start of the paragraph. The sentences that follow are formulated as if they are statements of the author himself, but because of the position in the text, it is clear that it still concerns a representation of Ankersmit's ideas. Whose voice is heard in a particular sentence thus can depend on the position of the sentence in the historical account. A statement from the example above – 'At most, the facts are the building blocks of the narrative, but which edifice is built with them, the historian, as architect of the narrative, decides himself' – placed in another position in Lorenz's argument would have been read as representing his own philosophy.

Because it must be clear for the historical debate exactly who holds which view, a proper division of paragraphs is very important. When the author discusses the ideas of another, at the very least the name of that other must be clearly stated, preferably in an obvious place, such as here at the beginning of the paragraph. As soon as the author leaves the ideas of his colleague and goes on to discuss his own views or those of a third historian, those ideas will require a new paragraph, the first sentence of which makes it clear whose ideas are being discussed.

paragraph division

4.4   Questions of style

Lastly, we shall deal briefly with three aspects of writing when the historian must make a conscious choice. These concern personal pronouns, the use of past and present tenses, and making specific or general statements.

4.4.1   Personal pronouns

In a historical account, the sentences usually have a neutral and business-like tone. As we explained previously, the author is always present in an academic text, but this is mostly an implicit presence that does not emerge from the style or sentence construction. Sometimes the author (as I or we) is explicitly present in the text, but it is preferable to avoid this style as much as possible. Often, the use of these personal pronouns is not necessary. The following construction, for instance, is often found in texts for prospective historians.

presence of the author

> The period after the Fourth Anglo-Dutch War (1780-1784) gives *us* a picture of growing social unrest, from which *we see that* the character, in particular in the last decade of the eighteenth century, was rapidly changing.

The sentence above is an adaptation of a sentence from a historical publication. In the original, the stylistic fault was not made. The reference to the reader and writer were not included. From it, it is evident that the addition of 'us' and 'we [see that]' were not necessary and moreover reduce the readability of the sentence.

> The period after the Fourth Anglo-Dutch War (1780-1784) gives a picture of growing social unrest, the character of which, in particular in the last decade of the eighteenth century, was rapidly changing.
>
> Taken from: Han Jordaan, *Slavernij & vrijheid op Curaçao. De dynamiek van een achttiende-eeuws Atlantisch handelsknooppunt* [*Slavery and freedom in Curaçao. The dynamics of an eighteenth-century trading hub*] (Zutphen 2013) 193. Our translation.

As well as the 'us/we' form (first person plural) in most academic texts, you should also avoid the use of the 'you' form (second person singular). This rule does not always apply: for instance, in an instructional text such as this book, the 'you' form has a function. A historical account does not have an instructional character, so 'you', 'us', and 'we' have no place in it. The more archaic form of 'one' should also be avoided. A sentence such as 'One often sees the first decade of the twentieth century as a period of new prosperity and development' can simply be rewritten as 'The first decade of the twentieth century is often seen as a period of new prosperity and development.' Incidentally, such a general statement needs a footnote to clarify who exactly sees it in this way or why it appears so.

'you', 'us', and 'we'

Other rules apply to the use of the 'I' form (first person singular). The historian's reflections on his or her own work which reveal the circumstances of the origins of the study can be useful, enabling the reader to understand the work better. Naturally, in such circumstances, the 'I' form does not need to be avoided. Such reflections are usually set in a part that is more or less separate from the main argument, such as the preface. In the argument itself, it is preferable to limit the use of 'I' to a minimum. An exception to this rule could be the emphatic discussion of a debate in which the author explicitly takes a position in regard to colleagues and therefore uses such constructions as 'I claim...' In the introduction to articles, the 'I' form is sometimes used in this way. Here, too, there is often a more impersonal form possible. 'In this article, I claim that...' can be rewritten as 'In this article, it is claimed that...' Due to the convention that the author is not emphatically present in a historical account, many readers prefer the second formulation. This is even better if, instead of using the passive voice, you can find an active alternative such as 'This article demonstrates that...'

'I' form

4.4.2   Past and present tenses

In general, writing about the past uses the past tense. Some guides to writ- *past tense*
ing state that writing in the present tense lends a lively tone to the text and
is therefore preferable. The sentence 'In 1939, the German army invades Po-
land' might sound lively, but here, the past tense 'invaded' is an accurate description and therefore is to be preferred in academic accounts of the past.

This does not mean that verbs in the present tense should be totally *present tense*
banned from historical accounts. When a historian addresses the historiography of a subject, he or she usually uses the present tense, as in the
following example:

> In his valedictory lecture, Jan Lucassen sketches a number of new per-
> spectives on the central insight that market economies 'not once, but se-
> veral times in history and in various places around the world [have] come
> into being, and in many cases also vanished.'

> Taken from: Van Rossum, *Werkers van de wereld [Workers of the world]*,
> 20. Our translation.

The valedictory lecture in question was already in the past at the time
of writing of this passage. Nevertheless, the choice was made to use the
present tense 'sketches' rather than 'sketched'. This was done because the
findings in this lecture are cited in the current debate on the subject (or
at least could be cited) and in that sense it is contemporary. By discussing
historiography in the present tense, the historian distinguishes between
the time of his or her historical subject and the time of the (present-day)
debate on that subject.

Past and present tenses can be used alternately in the same passage. *alternating tenses*
A finding about the past, written in the past tense, can be followed by a
remark about the consequences it has for the debate, written in the present tense. Such a construction would be something like: 'In the past, it
happened... This **gives rise** to the question...'

When describing a debate or a historiography, the present tense is not
always the best form. If the cited historian has passed away or in later
works no longer subscribes to the ideas discussed in the account, the past
tense is more suitable.

4.4.3   General and specific statements

The statements of historians about the past can be divided into two
categories: general and specific statements. General statements refer to *general statements*
the shared characteristics of various events. Specific statements refer to

unique events. The following description of the Netherlands in the 1950s is an example of a general statement:

> Traditional ideas about religion and morality were watched carefully by the authorities. The Dutch drew much of their identity from the consciousness of being a virtuous nation.
>
> Taken from: Hans van der Loo and Willem van Reijen, *Paradoxen van modernisering. Een sociaal-wetenschappelijke benadering* [*Paradoxes of modernisation. A social science approach*] (Third edition; Bussum 1997) 12. Our translation.

specific statements

These sentences do not refer to a specific moment that can be precisely localised in time and place but to a characteristic that was common to various times in the decade described. This is not the case with specific statements, as in the following citation:

> At the wedding on 10 March 1966, several smoke bombs exploded immediately behind the Golden Coach, which was then momentarily lost to sight.
>
> Taken from: Piet de Rooy, *Republiek van rivaliteiten. Nederland sinds 1813* [*Republic of rivalries. The Netherlands since 1813*] (Second, revised edition; Amsterdam 2005) 245. Our translation.

This sentence refers to a precise moment in the past. In the historical account, general statements are continually alternated with specific statements.

As a rule, historians strive for broad historical knowledge. Making general statements about the past is the primary aim of historical research. However, it should be noted that there are two concerns here. Firstly, general statements must be supported. No representation of the past is formed purely by generalities. Specific statements to support them are necessary to clarify and justify the general statements and therefore cannot be absent from a historical account. Secondly, general statements are always defined in a particular time and geographical context. A general statement about *designation of* the past is valid *within* that particular time frame and geographical context. *time and place* In the example above from the work of Van der Loo and Van Reijen, the general statement is valid for the Netherlands in the 1950s. Even if there is no reference to a unique event, the time and place must be given.

While historians are usually careful to define the period of time for their subject (the time frame), they sometimes neglect to delineate the geographical context. It is important to include the geographic area in which statements about the past are applicable. Continents, countries, kingdoms, and towns have geographic coordinates, but their designation is also historically determined (one 'Germany' is not another, for example). A geographic designation can also have a very substantive connotation, bound to culture or spheres of power and influence that imply geographic interplay, such as 'the Middle East conflict', 'Western science', or 'the influence of Rome in Latin America'. Explicitly reflecting on the geographic and substantive context in which the research takes place prevents implicit assumptions in regard to the range covered.

It is important to be cautious with the use of anaphora. Statements *anaphora* about the past – general or specific – should be able to stand on its own as much as possible. Replacing the subject of a sentence with an anaphor such as 'this' or 'that' can easily cause confusion. The problem arises in particular when reference is made to abstract historical processes. In such cases, you can prevent confusion simply by not replacing the subject of the sentence with an anaphor. When designating time, anaphora can also lead to a lack of clarity. It is better to avoid constructions such as 'a year later...' which cause the reader to turn back and read to see just which year is meant. In descriptions of the past, there is little that is as clear as giving the year.

A lot more can be said about writing a good text – the use of linking words to accurately indicate relations, avoiding obscure figures of speech such as complex, dependent clauses, tangential statements, and double negatives, etc. These questions are beyond the limits of the specialism of this chapter, which is aimed at the specific characteristics of an academic historical account. A good, general fluency in your mother tongue, English, and other languages is a very useful skill for every historian. There are several good writing guides available with tips about general linguistic points, and if they do not offer a sufficient basis, it could be useful to follow a course that caters to your specific needs in perfecting your written native language, English, or other language. Moreover, writing is exactly the sort of skill that is developed by doing it – repeatedly. One person learns more *skill comes with* quickly than the other, but practice undoubtedly increases writing skills. *practice*

4.4.4 Rules for annotation

Good historical research requires that anyone can check the data on which the historical work is based. To facilitate such checks, there are a number of accepted conventions in the discipline of history about style and referring to the sources that have been consulted for a historical account. These conventions ensure that every trained historian, when reading the work of a colleague, can immediately see where to find the information given – think of footnotes or endnotes, references to literature, mentions of institutions that hold archive items and sources such as images, tables, and figures.

various styles

These conventions are often referred to as rules for annotation. This does not mean rules in the literal sense. Different styles of notes can be found with different historians. Annotation rules have a purpose; above all, they are intended to improve the clarity for the reader concerning the nature of the information used and where to find it. In general, various annotation styles display great similarities. If each historian developed his or her own style of reference, finding the sources consulted would be a much more complex task for the reader, which is why academic disciplines have developed standards for annotation. This guide suggests, in the Dutch historiographic context, to use the annotation rules that were formulated in the manual by De Buck, Mout, Musterd, and Talsma.[3] These rules are the most important standard in Dutch-language history writing. The style is presented in detail in Appendix I.

images, graphs, and tables

It is not only important to have references to the right sources (and their location) or literature in a body text. Images, graphs, and tables should also have the proper source reference. Moreover, graphs and tables that you have produced yourself must be given a title that reflects the content in a clear and accurate way. This is often more difficult than it seems. By contrast to the body text, you should not use footnotes for images, etc. but instead place the source reference immediately below the image. Source references below the image follow similar rules as literature references. You should mention the maker of the image, the title, and lastly the location and the date of the making or publication. The location might be an archive, but it could just as well be a published source, such as an engraving in a book. As much specific information as possible such as the size and material of the original object, the holding institution, and/or the provenance should be added. See also Appendix I (1.8).

origins of images

A warning about references to the origins of images should be given. A great deal of pictorial material is available on the internet. It is important to realise that the website on which you find an image is not the original source. After all, websites make use of other people's images. They are not obliged to conform to the rules of academic referencing and it is therefore possible that the website does not provide a reference to the source of the image you want to use. In such a case, you will need to find out where the original image is located. This means that you can only mention a website as the source of an image if that image is published there for the first time. Moreover, it is important to realise that, in the case of images, there is often the question

copyrights

of copyright and that means that you cannot freely use every image in a publication. In addition, there are institutions, such as museums, that own such rights. If you want to publish a text with images, you must always check whether the images are free of such rights or if special permission (and sometimes payment) is required. The caption to the image should include the copyright sign, followed by the name of the holder of the copyright.

In principle, the use of graphs and tables is subject to the same rules as *graphs and tables* those for using images. When you use a table or graphs made by another author or institution, you must mention this under the graphs or table (according to the normal rules), including the maker, the source in which the figure is published, the year of publication, and the page number(s) where it is to be found. See Appendix I (1.9) for more details. As a historian, you will not only use tables and graphs made by others; when you do quantitative research, you must refer to the source(s) on which this research is based. In this case too, you should follow the usual annotation rules and render the archive items (or other sources) on which you have based your research correctly. Whether you have done your calculations from a database that you have set up yourself or one that has been created by others, you should mention the creator(s), the underlying sources and methods used to create the data. You can decide on the titles of graphs or tables yourself. Keep *titles* them brief and ensure that the title accurately reflects the contents of the figure. After all, the reader wants to know just what he or she is seeing. If applicable, always mention the correct dates, places, etc. For instance, if you are giving an overview of the number of *foreign* brides in the *betrothal registers* of *Amsterdam* between *1650 and 1800*, you need to make all these elements clear. It is also important to give the units (size, weight, numbers, currency) in which you express your data.

Notes

1 Hart, S., *Geschrift en getal. Een keuze uit de demografisch-, economisch- en sociaal-historische studiën op grond van Amsterdamse en Zaanse archivalia, 1600-1800* (Dordrecht 1976) 120-122, 135-144.

2 Taken from: J.R. McNeill and William H. McNeill, *The Human Web: A Bird's Eye View of World History* (New York and London 2003) 115.

3 P. de Buck et al., *Zoeken en schrijven. Handleiding bij het maken van een historisch werkstuk* (tenth edition, seventh printing; Baarn 2007).

Writing is a form of concentrated thinking that demands that the train of thought is made explicit. This chapter has demonstrated that it is also a technique that is very important for a convincing historical presentation. We also addressed the substantive aspects of the voice of the writer and the implicit or explicit debate in our handling of the text in general lines and at the level of paragraphs and sections. Lastly, we gave a brief explanation of annotation rules, which will be elaborated in Appendix I. The next chapter addresses the 'oral' variant of a good historical presentation. Speaking and writing are related to each other but have fundamental differences.

5 PRESENTATION AND HISTORICAL DEBATE

So far, the emphasis has been on writing history, but as we argued in Chapter 1, knowledge and insights into history are also advanced through discussions about the past. Historians are active listeners: they look around them, relate to those who have something to tell them, and respond with questions and points of view. Moreover, they are also used to presenting things themselves. You will notice how teachers enjoy working with a group of students and exploring a problem in more depth, but good teachers are also good speakers. They present a historical narrative with a beginning and an end in which unavoidably they place their own emphases or make their own selection by enlarging or omitting certain developments or events. No teacher just parrots a history book; depending on their audience, the narrative takes the form of an ongoing argument. This aspect of the discipline – talking about history and exchanging ideas about writing history – is part of the historian's training. Reports, papers, lectures, or posters are the four forms of oral presentation that we shall discuss below.

5.1   Form and style

The most important message of this chapter is that oral presentations are not one-way affairs. Such forms of communication and debate are excellent opportunities to exchange ideas with others and to obtain advice and comments that can then be used, either individually or as a group, to formulate new ideas. Talking about history is at the heart of the discipline.   *talking about history*

5.1.1   From working paper to poster presentation

Oral presentations can be found in many forms, and we will briefly discuss a few of them. A *working paper* is an oral presentation for a tutorial   *working paper*
group, prepared following a clear assignment. By a *paper*, we usually mean a written version of a lecture (paper presentation) given at a seminar,   *paper presentation*
symposium, or conference. A paper often has the same length as an article in a journal (between 6,000 and 12,000 words including the bibliography and source references). For an oral presentation, this written argument is usually reduced to 15 to 20 minutes, or 2,000 to 2,700 words. A *lecture*   *lecture*
can be just about anything: one rule of thumb is that the audience loses concentration after 50 minutes or so. Having said that, there are speakers who send people to sleep in five minutes while others make the audience forget the time and, after a short break, can hold the audience's attention even longer. It all depends on the nature of the subject, the speaker's technique and the context in which the lecture takes place.

Finally, a *poster* is a schematic, visualised summary of research or a research theme that allows the researcher to present the research in a brief *poster presentation* fashion that holds plenty of force or that can answer questions about the project from other researchers. Poster presentations during breaks at conferences and symposia are very common in the exact sciences and social sciences, and they are now finding their way into the humanities. There are, of course, countless other forms of oral presentation of historical research – quizzes, forum discussions, talk shows, documentaries, guided tours in museums, and so forth.

experience This variety of presentation forms underlines why prospective historians should not work only on their writing skills but also their presentation techniques. Presenting is a skill that comes with practice. Presenting regularly not only provides experience, it also teaches the speaker more about himself or herself better as regards a number of important aspects. For example, how do you respond to a large audience or to critical questions? How stressful do you find it to give a presentation? When do you feel that stress: during or just before your presentation? What are, for you, the best ways to cope with it?

5.1.2 Presentation styles

character of a presentation Determining the presentation style involves considering the context, the audience, and the aim of the presentation. A presentation can have the character of an *argument*, which is often the case when the speaker wants to convince an audience of colleagues of a particular position in a debate or of the importance of new or further research into a subject. In a working paper, you want to show that, in addition to having mastered the material, you have an active relationship with it – that you are able to take a position in regard to what you have read and found.

A presentation can also have an *informative* nature, for instance, to inform colleagues of the latest insights into a particular subject, to present a new book, or to explain how a research project was set up or to give information about (future) plans. Indeed, it is often a question of mixed forms, partly informative, partly argumentative – for example, when a presentation aims to convince the audience of the importance of developments in the past which have hitherto received insufficient attention. Lastly, a presentation can have the nature of an assessment when the speaker presents his/her hypotheses or research plans to an audience, either specialised or not, who can help by submitting comments and criticism.

If you look consciously, you will notice that historians use very different styles of presentation depending on their aims. Not everyone has the aptitude for all types of presentation. Some people are excellent at quizzes, while others if put in the same situation are unable to remember dates. Some prefer to talk more or less off the top of their heads and have enough structure with a PowerPoint or Prezi presentation; others need to write out the whole script to be certain that they have covered all the points of their argument. You really need to do a personal search for the way of giving a presentation that works best for you, and it is crucial that you remember the lessons from earlier presentations. It can be useful to keep notes of presentations with remarks about the good and bad points, questions that were asked, the length of your presentation, and how much it deviated from the guidelines. It can also be helpful to write a short evaluation after each presentation, with tips for the next time. *personal development* *evaluation*

Styles of presentation, such as 'off the top of your head' or 'written out', are not purely a question of talent but also have to do with how complex your story is, how far you are in the research process, whether what you are saying is very familiar to you or is still being developed, and how much you are confined by time limitations. Often a 'top of your head' style of speaking takes more time: you have more opportunity to search for words in interaction with your audience, repeat things to clarify them, or search for examples to illustrate an abstract statement. Remember that in that case, you must tell 'less', otherwise you will rapidly run out of time. Nothing puts people off more than a speaker who needs to gabble everything at the end because the moderator has tried to bring your talk to an end twice. If that happens, the audience will miss your conclusions. On the other hand, a talk that is written out can be 'thick' with information – exactly filling the time you have. However, if people come up to you afterwards and ask if they can read through it again, then you know that you have probably 'read' too much and 'communicated' too little. *'thickness' of the argument*

Whichever style you choose and however large your repertoire, every presentation demands preparation. A good preparation of a presentation takes into account an estimation of the audience, the surroundings, the nature of the presentation, and the type of debate you can expect. It is always sensible to estimate the size of your audience beforehand. A presentation to a large audience often has a more formal atmosphere than one held in a small, private space. A presentation in which you are judged, such as a working paper, differs from one in which you must 'draw in the audience', such as a poster presentation. It makes a great difference for your tone and style whether or not you are (partly) acquainted with people in the audience. *preparation*

If you are unable to estimate this yourself, for instance, if you are asked to speak at a meeting that you have not organised yourself, make sure that you contact the organisers beforehand to obtain important information such as the size of the audience, what sort of presentation is expected, how long you are expected to speak, the possibilities for having questions and a discussion after the talk, and any other expectations the organisers or audience might have of your presentation.

Adapt the way in which you prepare and shape your presentation in response to this information – the structure of your talk, aids, content. It is important to be aware that the purpose, the audience, and the context of your presentation are related to each other. For instance, certain parts of your research will have more appeal to an audience with a more general interest in history than they would to a specialist audience of colleagues. Explain specialist terms or theories to an audience for whom such knowledge is not self-evident, but never underestimate your audience. Nothing is as annoying to an audience as having the feeling that they are not being taken seriously.

5.1.3   A few tips and guidelines

Below, we give a few practical tips for the preparation of a presentation concerning: (a) eliciting interaction, (b) preventing technical problems, and (c) the structure of your oral argument.

(a) Ensuring interaction with your audience

It almost goes without saying that you should think beforehand about how your audience will receive you. That concerns your use of language (Dutch, English or another language) and also the way you speak. Certainly, if you are not used to speaking in a foreign language, it is advisable to read your text aloud beforehand and underline and make other notations in your text for pronunciation and rhythm. Think about how you should approach your audience; should you address them formally or informally? Exactly which words will you use, and what will be their effect on your listeners? If you really want interaction, it is a good idea to build questions into your presentation. If you do, consider whether you use a rhetorical question, to which you do not really expect an answer, or one that can stimulate the audience to give their views. And on the subject of interaction, think about your clothing: should it be formal or informal – or something in-between? It is also important to consider how you feel in your clothes. If you feel comfortable in them, you will give a better presentation; or perhaps you will if you dress a little more formally than usual. Everybody is different in this respect, and it is important to find your own preferences.

built-in questions

(b) Preventing technical problems

It can be useful to include elements that give a degree of flexibility – for example, extra examples or digressions that you can omit during the presentation if it becomes evident that you do not have enough time. It is also handy, if you have a PowerPoint or Prezi presentation that supports your talk, to have slides with extra information on hand, such as tables, graphs, or maps that are not necessary in your presentation but could be useful for a round of questions or a discussion. If you arrange these slides to follow after the final slide of the regular (PowerPoint) presentation, you can bring them out if the audience has questions relating to this extra information, which substantiates your argument but has not been included in the presentation due to time pressure.

Various textual and visual aids can be used to support a presentation. *tools and aids* We have already mentioned PowerPoint and Prezi presentations. In a PowerPoint presentation, you 'flip' from slide to slide: in a Prezi presentation, you can show the whole story as an image, line, or map and then zoom in on the subsequent details of this *overall* image. Textual and visual support works best if the slides are not overcrowded, the font size is big enough, and the visual material is of a good quality for projection. Make sure that the visual material has the proper captions: for a painting, for *captions* instance, give the name of the painter, the title, date, material, size, and the collection in which it can be found (see 2.3.3 (d)). Accordingly, the images add force to your argument instead of being 'a picture' added to history, as argued in Chapter 3.

More and more frequently, interactive projection screens are available on which you can extend or change the slides during the presentation – this is more suitable for workshop-type situations or tutorial groups than for plenary sessions in which the speaker should not be like a disc jockey, always busy with technical matters. You can simply prepare a number of hyperlinks to click through to digital maps, websites, film material, *hyperlinks* music, and suchlike. The programmes available for this are continually developing and have acquired their own specific advantages and disadvantages. Whatever you use, ask about the technical possibilities before- *technology available* hand: is there a beamer or projector at the location? Do the computers that are needed for your presentation have the right programming? Is it perhaps necessary to bring your own laptop, and can it be linked to the beamer or projector? Is there an internet connection (for things like film material or interactive maps), and can that connection be made without too much fuss? If you have prepared properly, you should have clarity on these points well before you give your presentation. Build in an extra level of certainty by ensuring that you have a back-up of your presentation or simply taking an earlier train if the presentation is in another town. Install your presentation on the computer well before your talk begins and check that it works and is not distorted by a different version of the software. You lose your audience's attention if they have to sit through ten minutes of you trying to get your presentation on the screen. If it does go wrong, make sure you have a 'plan B' without audio-visual support, or, if *plan B* necessary, a printed handout.

Keep the situation under control and do not begin making excuses *giving your* and providing *disclaimers*: this will give a poor impression. This applies *presentation* not only to technical problems. People who are uneasy or think (or even have experienced) that their expertise is not easily accepted are more inclined to apologise – claiming that they have only just started with this subject, had too little time to prepare, or perhaps do not have enough to contribute. Do not do that! Stand firm, take a deep breath, stand up straight, trust in your good preparations, and leave the final judgement to your audience. Sometimes you must choose whether to speak standing or sitting. Sitting down might seem more natural and accessible, but standing is often best. You create a better point of focus for your audience; you can better judge your stance and breathing, and you are free in your movements – walking back and forth to point out something on a slide, wave your arms in the heat of your argument, emphatically indicate someone to give their view, look at the moderator, etc. Even if all the speakers before you remained seated, do not hesitate to stand. No-one will think it strange, and it can give a bit of essential variety to the occasion.

(c) Rules of thumb for the structure of your argument

Every presentation has its own form, aim, and depth. Nevertheless, there are a few rules of thumb for the content and structure, comparable to *content and structure* the structure and content of a historical essay presenting an argument or information. If the moderator does not introduce you, begin your story with a short introduction of yourself and present your subject in one sentence, giving your talk a telling title and explaining it very briefly. Then, again very briefly (and possibly accompanied by a slide), you should present the parts of your talk – introduction, presentation 1, 2, 3, etc., conclusion – that you designate with appropriate subtitles (referring perhaps to periodisation or developments in your subject). Please note, do this in proportion to the length of time you have to speak: a 20-minute paper should have the briefest of introductions, while a 50-minute lecture can use a fairly thorough one. Whether short or long, after giving the 'contents', take a breath and then begin the main talk. Take a moment's break ('Now I come to the next part...') for each subtitle so that your audience can follow the thread of your argument. Also say explicitly, 'lastly / in conclusion, the following...' or 'to sum up, I have argued that...' The audience now knows that you have reached the end and will pay extra attention. This ensures that they do not miss anything, such as a handy summary or a daring conclusion, and they can consider your whole argument.

The structure of your presentation will be stronger if you practise your talk in the following three ways: first use keywords that indicate various elements and that lead to a conclusion (also expressed in keywords); then practise with a full written text; and finally give your talk with images and slides. Before your presentation, spend time just walking around with the full talk in your head and try to reconstruct the building blocks (tell *remembering the* yourself a few times, 'First, I say this, then that, and then I come to that'). *building blocks* Sometimes, it helps if you literally walk round to help memorise your argument. Classical rhetoric developed all kinds of techniques whereby a speaker could fix a speech in his mind by linking this to a spatial situation furnished with certain objects – for instance, the rooms of a house. In your thoughts, you go from place to place and what you see in your mind's eye you associate with what you want to say. In a guided tour of *guided tour* an exhibition, the guide talks quite literally from what there is to see and how his group moves through the rooms. In a lecture, where the audience sits still and the speaker and audience can only be drawn into the story in their minds, the Prezi presentation is a modern digital version of the old rhetorical principle (the PowerPoint presentation is closer to the tradition of a book, where one turns the pages). Whatever the manner, if you can reproduce your argument for yourself, this will also reinforce the structure of the textual, visual, and auditory support of your talk.

5.2   Feedback and debate

In smaller groups, you can build up a fully interactive presentation more easily, but with a working paper in a tutorial group or another formal or larger meeting, it is common for there to be time set aside after the pres- entation for comments and questions. Historians are well practised in *commentary and* debate and in both giving and receiving comments. *questions*

In addition to speaking, giving comments is an indispensable skill for a historian. Good comments highlight both the strong and weak points of an argument and the research that lies behind it. First, men- tion a number of positive things. This is more than just being kind: it is an indispensable form of feedback. To improve the work, the speaker *feedback* must know explicitly what went well. Improvements must be embed- ded in that which is to be retained. Moreover, it makes the positive or strong points of the argument clear to both the speaker and the audi- ence. After that, it is time to turn to the problem points. Do not be worried about mentioning these: everyone needs criticism to progress. *criticism* Make sure the criticism is substantive and gets to the heart of the way the subject is handled. Criticism must also be constructive: it is a posi- tive action that should help the speaker. Therefore, formulate your criti- cism in a professional and constructive manner. Criticism must never be personal. You should also provide (clues for) solutions to the prob- lems you point out and give useful advice to the speaker which he or she can use in future.

referent   Often, the first to offer a comment is an expert or other commentator (referent) who has prepared a response. The aim of this sort of commentary is to encourage discussion of the subject and to highlight the strong and weak points of the argument. The referent sometimes confirms the importance of the presentation or points out important aspects of the context (for example, how the talk fits into the overall theme of the meeting). It is important that the commentator can prepare as well as possible. This makes the commentary not only better but also more useful as feedback for the speaker. When the presentation is related to a text or research project, it is customary to send all the relevant documents to the commentators beforehand. You might expect this for a paper, a research plan, or a provisional working paper or article.

5.2.1   Critique and support

commentary   Depending on the expertise and the role of the referent, the comments are directed at various aspects of what has been presented. With the presentation of a research plan, it could be directed, for example, at the delimitation and aim of the proposed research. Does the speaker want to do too much, or perhaps too little? Is the research directed at the most crucial or interesting subject or the right research question? There might also be criticism on the connection between the research question and the proposed methodology. Will this specific manner of research produce answers, or could a different approach to the same source be more profitable? An important area of commentary is that of conclusions and interpretations. Do the research results really indicate the conclusions made? Is it possible they could indicate something else?

Referents who respond to research that has been completed or is in a more advanced stage often choose another strategy in response to a talk. They complement the arguments of the speaker with their own example of a specific case study that supports, modifies, or contradicts the general argument and to which the speaker must respond. Such a reaction must be well prepared. After all, the referent has much less time than the first speaker and can only sketch his or her 'counterexample' in broad lines.

statements and   Both criticism, advice, and other approaches can be formulated as an-
questions   nouncements – emphatic statements, perhaps more emphatic because of the discussion – but also in the form of questions. These two forms affect the debate in different ways. A question can have the effect of stimulating both the speaker and audience to think about a particular part of the presentation and perhaps even to brainstorm, whereby new ideas and insights come into being. It is therefore a pity when the referent asks a good question but can add little to it – the more background the questioner has, the more interesting the ensuing debate will be. Criticism, advice,

or alternatives in the form of emphatic statements, if coupled with some supporting evidence, create more clarity and can therefore underline the urgency of the commentary.

A historian will have learned to give a presentation and to take part in a debate. As with a presentation, it is important with feedback to consider beforehand the what and the how – the manner in which the comments are formulated. Less important advice (language usage, manner of presentation, use of page numbers, or other minor details) can be given in writing or dealt with very briefly. This gives sufficient room for comments to concentrate as much as possible on the important points of criticism, questions, and advice. Do not just sit back after you have given your comments: comments help a speaker and stimulate further thought. Often *comments help* they serve to open up a broader round of discussion in which the referent *the speaker* is partly responsible for a fruitful outcome.

Having addressed how to ask questions (Chapter 1), how to present primary and secondary sources (Chapter 2), how to use those sources (Chapter 3), and how to write (Chapter 4), this chapter gave a brief discussion of the final element of the historian's craft: how to lecture and debate. Historians should, above all, be trained to interpret and provide a context. Each individual must decide for him or herself what he or she will do with these foundations. Chapter 6 concludes this companion by discussing the opportunities for prospective historians.

6 A HISTORIAN – NOW WHAT?

This guide for prospective historians stresses the understanding and skills that are essential for the historian's craft. During your time at university, you will become involved in that craft for the first time. The structure of the course includes the fundamental parts of a historian's job as well as practice situations in which current knowledge is transferred by means of reference works, exams, and seminars but also research situations in which new historical knowledge is generated. It is generated in tutorials, by means of presentations, papers, theses, lectures, or seminars. Regard your course as a way to practise history, not as a 'preliminary stage' for that practice. Universities are places where history is written, and students contribute to it while acquiring the ins and outs of the job. Students are part of the academic community and are more than welcome to join in activities related to the field by attending lectures by guest speakers, the inauguration speeches of newly appointed professors, dissertation defences and the like.

6.1   Professional opportunities

What kind of job does a historian have, actually? Depending on their disposition and their academic careers, historians are trained to be either practical or contemplative and are highly regarded intellectuals with a wide range of skills. A Bachelor programme, whether or not it is combined with a minor focused on teaching or another career, is a fully rounded course that in theory prepares people for the realities of a profession. A Master's degree programme and a Research Master's programme provide historians with further qualifications. Moreover, the Research Master's programme prepares students for a potential future job as a researcher who works on a dissertation. Historians can often be employed in many fields, including education, journalistic writing, broadcasting companies, ICT companies, museums and the heritage sector, publishing, tourism, government agencies, non-government organisations, or more commercial businesses. Some historians become politicians, union leaders, or governors, while others move into writing novels. Needless to say, this list of possible careers is by no means complete.

practical, contemplative, having an opinion

capable of working in a wide range of fields

Based on their study of and knowledge about the past, historians relate to their fellow historians, both in writing and orally, and to society as a whole. And, depending on the subject, there is scope for historians to give their opinions on current affairs. Nonetheless, historians are not oracles who can explain the present or predict the future: if they do – which is fine, of course, and likely to raise a debate – the views expressed will usually be political views. After all, even ministers or CEOs, who have good advisers (including historians) do not have any guarantees for the consequences of their decisions. Historians will often be invited to participate in a panel or to join an opinion programme or a political gathering. For such things, historians are extremely well suited, but they seldom take on the role of Cassandra's oracle. In most cases, they are cautious about making any 'historical judgement'.

career

Because historians are trained in a wide range of fields and have often learned many skills that are generally useful and can draw on many talents, it can be difficult to decide on a career path from the very first. Moreover, a career path often requires some intermediary steps such as taking a teaching course for qualifications to teach in secondary education after obtaining a Master's degree, a (paid) traineeship with the government or a commercial party, courses that focus on specific jobs, in-service training with a company, etc. A career depends not only on your choices or ambitions to reach your goals, the economic situation obviously also influences your chances of finding work.

History graduates are equipped for a wide range of jobs. Even if, in the end, your work has little to do with historical research, it can still lead to personal enrichment if you continue to regard yourself as a historian and continue to stay informed about and question the processes in which you are involved. It is the quality, knowledge, and skills that contribute to the standard of your work. Even historians who have found work in other fields are often still active in historical organisations such as local history societies, the Royal Netherlands Historical Society (the professional association for historians), or in reading clubs that stay up to date with the literature. History is a field in which you can stay actively involved, even if you are not employed in it.

'active' study

Since the purpose of studying history is to make you a proficient historian by taking part in the academic practice of history, you will get the most out of your studies if you study in an active way and try out all sorts of paths. Explore what your interests are, and what kinds of talents you have. What excites you? What aspects or which periods of history are you most interested in, and what do you think you can do with it 'later'? What should you do if you want to explore this further? The tools you need are incorporated into your study, but the opportunities outside your study are just as important. You can discover them by looking for work experience and doing traineeships or committee work (the latter could be at the university or somewhere else), which allow you to discover what interests you, what you are good at, and what you would rather avoid. You will learn other things than you can learn in your course, and perhaps you will even acquire some specific competences, certificates, or qualifications.

Preparing for your future after your time at university should, in a certain sense, focus on finding a balance between two factors: interests and opportunities. This search is not without obligations. A thorough understanding of your own interests and qualities can be gained by testing them, in other words, by actually doing something with the interests and qualities you think you have. Take yourself and those around you seriously. A vague notion such as 'I'd like to go abroad' is usually not enough to get you abroad. Go and investigate, set yourself challenges, and take advantage of all the support and advice you can get during your time at university: from your course, your fellow students, and the organisations you want to join. Most historians presumably find salaried employment after they graduate, while others go freelance (self-employed), and in reality, many students will start working before they leave university.

preparing for the future

If you can, be critical in the few years you are allowed for your studies, focus your energy as much as you can on finding work that is – even only slightly – connected to your study. There are all sorts of financial options available available for students to acquire experience abroad – for example, during your course – or for doing traineeships with institutions where you might like to work. Traineeships and work experience projects are important tools for exploring your own interests and qualities but will also smooth your path to (a specific sector of) the employment market. If all is well, you should feel challenged to put specific academic and historical skills into practice such as analysing complex issues, considering the relationship between cause and effect, prioritising important parts of certain duties, writing clear reports, or reporting in person. At the same time, you will learn new skills such as assessing an issue based on certain non-academic but organisational, commercial, or social criteria, maintaining a professional network, and other forms of job-related discipline. While doing traineeships and working, you will not only acquire new skills, you will also meet new people with whom you can build a network that may help you find a job after graduating. Moreover, during your traineeship or work experience, you will get an impression of how that particular organisation works – what is thought important and what not. It will help you form a better idea of the work you would like to do, but also tell you whether you would be suited to work in that organisation or not.

traineeships and work experience

building networks

6.2   The importance of publishing

core skills Lastly, doing research and writing are important core skills for historians. If you publish, you are not only sharing your knowledge and insights, you are also proving that you have a command of research and writing skills, that you can produce fully rounded final results, and that you have the ambition to be an active historian. Sometimes, you may even manage to use good research you have done during your study for publication. Many people also gain experience during their course by writing a review, a popular scientific article, a weblog, or an op-ed article. If you would like to continue in this way after graduation, don't leave it too late and think carefully about the relationship between your
choice of media aim and the best medium for your intended text. Usually, an op-ed is published in a daily newspaper, but this requires that your argument has a certain topicality or urgency. More specific arguments or expositions that could be relevant for a certain professional group might perhaps be better submitted to a trade journal. The same applies to reviews and articles: choose a suitable journal and get in touch with the editors before you get to work so that you know whether they are in theory willing to feature the review. More general or popular-historical texts are often more suitable for corresponding magazines or websites. Here again, it might be a good idea to discuss your idea with the editors first.

And don't underestimate the fact that the research results of your Master's thesis and the like are potentially interesting and novel enough
academic publication to incorporate them into an academic publication. Perhaps your tutor will point such things out to you, or vice versa; if you are considering publication but feel uncertain about it, just ask. There are some really good books and articles that contain adaptations of theses or papers. An adaptation for an academic publication usually means that you must set out your case with more force and follow a more rigid structure – it should present the results rather than report the research process. This 'revision exercise' is all part of the job – and you will soon find how much satisfaction can be gained from seeing your research published. Almost every publisher and every journal will require that your manuscript is first accepted by the editors as having potential interest and will then be
peer review reviewed (anonymously) by third parties. The comments on your article will be put into a clear-cut report, with a conclusion as to whether or not it is suitable for publication (perhaps with revisions). Make an assessment, beforehand (or ask your lecturers advice) as to whether an article is suitable for a particular journal, and then examine the requirements the journal sets for articles and for its layout and presentation. The rules and guidelines that apply 'in real life' do not deviate, or do

not deviate fundamentally, from the rules and guidelines that are part of your academic training. Perhaps this companion can therefore even prove useful after you graduate. And who knows, perhaps by then this guide proves to be outdated, while you choose with confidence your own path in writing history.

APPENDICES

APPENDIX I
GUIDELINES FOR NOTES

This appendix contains a brief list of the most common rules (or guidelines) for annotating references to various kinds of literature and sources when writing a historical text. *Writing History!* follows the rules for annotation from the older Dutch manual of De Buck, Mout, Musterd, and Talsma.[1] This 'De Buck style' is also used by Dutch historical journals such as the BMGN – *Low Countries Historical Review* and *Tijdschrift voor Geschiedenis*. A 'De Buck format' has been developed for EndNote. When you read through the examples, make sure you pay attention to the punctuation: all full stops, commas, semi-colons, and colons are part of the style.

I.1 Referring to the literature, websites, sources

I.1.1 Referring to a book

A reference to a book should contain, in consecutive order, the author's name, the title (in italics), and the town and year in which the book was published (in brackets). This information can be found on the title page and reverse of the book's title page. The reference should follow the spelling used in the title on the title page. An exception to this rule is the use of capital letters. In Dutch historical writing, the custom is to only use capitals for words in the title for which they would be used in an ordinary sentence, regardless of the use of capitals on the title page of the book itself. If a book has a subtitle, it should form a new sentence in the reference. The same applies to the spelling of the author's name: it should correspond to the name on the title page. Sometimes an author's full first name is given, while in other cases only the initials of the author's first name(s) are given. In notes, the author's name should also be spelled as it is given on the title page.

For example, if you are using the original edition of Johan Huizinga's Herfsttij der Middeleeuwen [The Waning of the Middle Ages], you should refer to it as follows:

> J. Huizinga, *Herfsttij der Middeleeuwen. Studie over levens- en gedachten-vormen der veertiende en vijftiende eeuw in Frankrijk en de Nederlanden* (Haarlem 1919).

However, few people have the first edition of Huizinga's famous work, which was published in 1919 by H.D. Tjeenk Willink of Haarlem. You will not often come across the aforementioned reference. If you refer to a later edition, you do not include the year and town of the original edition but rather those of the version you consulted. This is necessary because page numbers can deviate per edition, so if you refer to a certain page, it is essential to mention which version of the book you used. You must also state exactly which edition it is. References to the first ten editions are written in letters, as in De Buck, whom we quoted on page 133: 'Tenth edition, seventh printing'. After ten editions, the number is given in numerals. The information about the edition should be given before the place it was published, separated by a semi-colon.

If, for instance, you rely on the 33rd edition of Huizinga's book, published in 2012 by Olympus in Amsterdam, you use the following reference:

> J. Huizinga, *Herfsttij der Middeleeuwen. Studie over levens- en gedachten-*
> *vormen der veertiende en vijftiende eeuw in Frankrijk en de Nederlanden*
> (33rd edition; Amsterdam 2012).

If you make a reference to a specific passage, a page number should follow
the reference:

> J. Huizinga, *Herfsttij der Middeleeuwen. Studie over levens- en gedachten-*
> *vormen der veertiende en vijftiende eeuw in Frankrijk en de Nederlanden*
> (33rd edition; Amsterdam 2012) 95.

Not every author makes the same choices for the notes in a text as regards the spelling of titles in other languages. As it is customary in English-speaking academic circles to capitalise almost all words in the title
(except for articles, prepositions, and conjunctions), some authors use
this style when they refer to a work in English. In the same way, the subtitle is not introduced as a new sentence but with a colon following the
main title, as is the custom in English-speaking academic circles. Other
authors choose to refer to English titles in the notes of a Dutch text in
the Dutch way. As a consequence, the same reference can be given in two
different ways:

> S. Shapin and S. Schaffer, *Leviathan and the air-pump. Hobbes, Boyle, and*
> *the experimental life* (Princeton 1985).

> S. Shapin and S. Schaffer, *Leviathan and the Air-Pump: Hobbes, Boyle,*
> *and the Experimental Life* (Princeton 1985).

The author must decide how he or she wants to capitalise words when
referring to titles in other languages. However, once decided, he or she
must apply it consistently throughout the text. If an English title is written the 'Dutch way', it should apply to all English titles. The same applies,
of course, if you decide to use the 'Anglo-Saxon' method of annotation.
If you choose to write English titles using the Anglo-Saxon method, the
Dutch titles should nevertheless be reproduced in the Dutch way. Accordingly, the following two references may be found in the notes of the
same work:

> Donald R. Kelly, *Frontiers of History: Historical Inquiry in the Twentieth*
> *Century* (New Haven 2006).
> J.N. Bakhuizen van den Brink et al., *Geschiedenis. Een bundel studies over*
> *den zin der geschiedenis* (Assen 1944).

If you make a reference to a translated work, you must give the transla-tor's name between the title and the place it was published, preceded by the abbreviation **transl.** (in Dutch: **vert.**):

> Karl R. Popper, *De armoede van het historicisme*, transl. G. van Benthem van den Bergh (Amsterdam 1967).

A translation should be provided for titles in languages other than Dutch, English, French, or German. It should be in brackets and follow the title of the work. The place and year of publication should follow a semi-colon.

> Wu Yujin and Qi Shirong, *Shijie Shi* (Wereldgeschiedenis; Beijing 1994).

If a book is one of a series, the name of the series may be included in the reference. The name of the series is given after the book's title. However, in many references, the series is not mentioned.

> Frank McDonough, *The Origins of the First and Second World Wars*. Cambridge Perspectives in History (Cambridge 1997).

If you refer to a published source such as a diary, the original author is named first. The editor of the contemporary edition is given after the title, followed by the abbreviation **ed.**

> Samuel Pepys, *The illustrated Pepys: extracts from the diary*. Robert Lat-ham ed. (London 1978).

Once you have referred to a certain title, you can shorten it in subsequent references. Now, the author's surname will suffice.

> Huizinga, *Herfsttij der Middeleeuwen*.

And a reference to a page number:

> Huizinga, *Herfsttij der Middeleeuwen*, 95.

If you make a reference to information that can be found on several pages, it should be mentioned in the same reference, separated by a comma. If you refer to an entire chapter or passage that covers several pages, note the first and last page of the passage, separated by a hyphen. So, if you refer to the entire passage from page 66 to page 75, and to the separate page 106, you should reproduce it as:

> Huizinga, *Herfsttij der Middeleeuwen*, 66-75, 106.

If a book is published in two places at the same time, both places should be mentioned in the reference, separated by a semi-colon or hyphen. In Dutch publications, the word 'and' (in Dutch: 'en') is often used instead. If more than three places are mentioned on the title page, the reference only includes the first place, followed by the abbreviation **etc.**: (London etc.1984).

> Herbert Schnadelbach, *Geschichtsphilosophie nach Hegel. Die Probleme des Historismus* (Freiburg; Munich 1974).
> M. Bentley, *Modern historiography. An introduction* (London-New York 2003).

If the title page does not mention a year or place of publication, you mark the absence in the reference with the abbreviation **n.d.** (no date) (in Dutch: **z.j.**) or **n.p.** (no place) (in Dutch: **z.p.**). Such abbreviations are placed where you would normally put the place or year.

If a book has two or more authors, they should all be mentioned in the first reference, but it suffices in subsequent references to give the name of the first author, followed by the Latin abbreviation *et al.* (and others) (in Dutch: **e.a.**).

If a book has more than three authors, only the first author is mentioned in the first reference. In the latter case, the bibliography at the end of the text, in which all the literature you have consulted is listed, includes all the authors by name.

> J.R. McNeill and William H. McNeill, *The human web. A bird's-eye view of world history* (New York 2003).
> P. de Buck et al., *Zoeken en schrijven. Handleiding bij het maken van een historisch werkstuk* (Haarlem 1982).

And the shorter version:

> McNeill et al., *The human web*.
> P. de Buck et al., *Zoeken en schrijven*.

l.1.2   Referring to an article in a journal

Just as in the case of titles of books, the punctuation for articles from journals must be accurate too. A reference to an article in a journal should contain, in this order:

- the author's name
- the title of the article (between quotation marks)
- the name of the journal (in italics)
- the volume number of the journal number (which usually consists of the year of publication and the part of that volume)
- the year of publication
- the page numbers within which the article can be found in the journal.

> Elizabeth Edwards, 'Photographic Uncertainties: Between Evidence and Reassurance', *History and Anthropology* 25:2 (2014) 171-188.

Or, following the Dutch way:

> Elizabeth Edwards, 'Photographic uncertainties: between evidence and reassurance', *History and Anthropology* 25:2 (2014) 171-188.

Remember that, in the latter case, the words in the journal's title are capitalised too. If you refer to one or more specific pages of an article, you should provide them after stating the page numbers taken up by the article in the journal, preceded by a comma and the abbreviation 'q.v.'. (in Dutch: 'aldaar').

> Elizabeth Edwards, 'Photographic uncertainties: between evidence and reassurance', *History and Anthropology* 25:2 (2014), 171-188, q.v. 178.

In a similar fashion to references to a book, the second and later references to an article in a journal are given in a shorter version:

> Edwards, 'Photographic uncertainties'.

And stating the page number:

> Edwards, 'Photographic uncertainties', 178.

I.1.3   Referring to an article in a collection

A reference to an article in a collection should contain, in this order:
- the author of the article
- the title of the article (between quotation marks)
- the editor of the collection
- the title of the collection
- the place and year of publication
- the page numbers where the article can be found in the collection.

There should be no comma between the title of the article and the author of the collection, as is the case with a reference to an article in a journal, but you should add the word 'in' followed by a colon. The name of the author of the collection is followed by the abbreviation **ed.** (or in Dutch: **red.**), which stands for editor (in Dutch 'redacteur'). If there are several editors, the abbreviation **eds.** (or in Dutch: **red.**) is used.

> J.C. Kennedy, 'Religion, Nation and European Representations of the Past' in: Stefan Berger and Chris Lorenz eds., *The Contested Nation: Ethnicity, Class, Religion and Gender in National Histories* (Basingstoke 2008) 104-134.

A reference to one or more specific pages in the article should be given in the same way as you would give to an article in a journal:

> J.C. Kennedy, 'Religion, Nation and European Representations of the Past' in: Stefan Berger and Chris Lorenz eds., *The Contested Nation: Ethnicity, Class, Religion and Gender in National Histories* (Basingstoke 2008) 104-134, q.v. 108-109.

And the shorter version, with page numbers:

> Kennedy, 'Religion, Nation', 108-109.

A reference to a collection in its entirety is almost the same as a reference to a book. If you are referring to a collection, you should follow your reference with the abbreviation **ed.** or **eds.** (or in Dutch: **red.**) after the names, to indicate that you are talking about editors and to emphasise that others contributed to the work.

> Stefan Berger and Chris Lorenz eds., *The Contested Nation: Ethnicity, Class, Religion and Gender in National Histories* (Basingstoke 2008)

If the writer of the particular article you are referring to happens to be the editor of the collection, the name of the editor is replaced by the word 'Idem'.

> Geoffrey Roberts, 'J.H. Hexter: Narrative History and Common Sense' in: Idem, *The History and Narrative Reader* (London and New York 2001) 135-139.
> J.C.H. Blom, '"Durch kamen sie doch". Het Nederlands defensiebeleid in de jaren dertig opnieuw beschouwd' in: Idem, *Crisis, bezetting en herstel. Tien studies over Nederland 1930-1950* (The Hague 1989) 37-55.

If a collection is put together by a large group of editors whose names are too many to put on the title page, the reference should not include the authors' names.

> *Wetenschap en rekenschap, 1880-1980. Een eeuw wetenschapsbeoefening en wetenschapsbeschouwing aan de Vrije Universiteit* (Kampen 1980).

The rules for referring to an article in a collection also apply to books of which a reprint has been published in a collection of works by the author. You should place the title of the original book, now between quotation marks, after the name of the author. This should be followed by the year of the original edition of the individual work in brackets, which in turn should be followed by the author and title of the collected work, the place and year of publication, and the page numbers in the collected works.

> Robert Fruin, 'Over het bewaren van het lijk voor het proces bij de Friezen' (1886) in: Idem, *Verspreide Geschriften* VIII (The Hague 1903) 147-148.

I.1.4 Referring to a website or digitally available source

A reference to a website should contain the name of the website, the URL and, between brackets, the date on which you most recently consulted the website. The latter detail is necessary, as the content of a website is subject to change.

> Internet Encyclopedia of Philosophy – A Peer-Reviewed Academic Resource, www.iep.utm.edu/ (consulted 23 August 2014).

If you consult a book, a chapter, or an article online, you should, when you refer to it, render the full title description followed by the URL and (between brackets) the date on which you consulted the digital or digitalised text. The URL alone is never sufficient. If there is also a 'hard copy' of the text, the usual reference will suffice, if you are sure that the digital version does not deviate from it.

More and more articles that are available online also state the DOI number (Digital Object Identifier). If you add the DOI to the address bar of your internet browser after http://dx.doi.org/, the file in question can be found directly. The advantage of the DOI is that the article can be found in the long-term future by these means, even if the actual internet address is changed. The DOI should be given after the reference.

> Karel Davids, 'River Control and the Evolution of Knowledge: A Comparison Between Regions in China and Europe, c. 1400-1850', *Journal of Global History* 1:1 (March 2006) 59-79. DOI: 10.1017/S1740022806000040.

I.1.5   Referring to an archival item

The rules for referring to an archival item are not as strict as the rules for referring to a printed source. Generally speaking, the details of the location of the source become increasingly detailed.

- First of all, the institute holding the item (the archives, documentary institution, library, or museum) is given, usually followed by the place in which it is accommodated.
- If that authority is divided into branches or departments, you must include the branch or department that keeps the item, as long as that information is relevant to finding the item.
- Next, you should state the name of the archives or the collection to which the item belongs.When we say 'archives' here, we mean a cohesive collection of items and not the institution that looks after the items, which are also often called 'archives' (such as the Nationaal Archief in The Hague). You have, of course, already mentioned that institution. Sometimes, archives are numbered, and the archive number can be placed after the name of the archive, between brackets. The archive number should not be confused with the inventory number.
- Next, you should state the inventory number, preceded by the abbreviation **inv.no.** (in Dutch: **inv.nr.**). This is then followed by the title, if any, of the specific item or a brief description of the item (a few words). If the date on which the item was prepared is known, it should be added.
- If the item is in a numbered volume, you might need to include a folio number, preceded by the abbreviation **f.**. If both sides of the paper were written on and the relevant piece only covers one side, put **r.** (for 'recto' = front) or **v.** (for 'verso' = reverse).

Here are some examples:[2]

> University Library Leiden, Archive K.H. Roessingh (BPL 2825), inv.no. 22, lecture 'Troeltsch' (1915).
> University Library Groningen, Archive G. van der Leeuw (not in inventory), K.H. Roessingh to G. van der Leeuw, 17 June 1919.
> University Library Nijmegen, KDC, Archive A.G. Weiler, inv.no. 59, untitled letter, 16 January, 1969.
> National Archives The Hague, ICWO Archive, 2.20.34.1, Minutes of ICWO meeting 26 November 1896.

The abbreviation 'BPL' in the first example is a signature that is linked to the number of the archive in question by the institution that keeps the archives (the University Library in Leiden). That signature refers to the person from whom, or the institution from which, the archive comes. In this case, 'BPL' refers to Collectie Bibliotheca Publica Latina.

Archives or archive items are rendered in a shorter version in later references, which can be done by abbreviating the name of the institution that holds the archives. That abbreviation should be put between brackets following the full name of the institution that holds the archives in the first reference or presented at the back before the bibliography. In later references, you only need to use the abbreviation. Common Dutch abbreviations are NA (formerly: RA) for National Archives (Nationaal Archief) (formerly: Rijksarchief or State Archives) and GA for Gemeentearchief (Municipal Archives). If you refer to sources from a museum or an institution, you can also use abbreviations, e.g. RMA for Rijksmuseum Amsterdam, B&G for Nederlands Instituut voor Beeld en Geluid (Netherlands Institute for Sound and Vision).

Because the rules for referring to archives are not so clear-cut, in order to avoid confusion, the author may state, in the first reference, how he or she will abbreviate the archive in later references.

> University Library Gent, Department of Manuscripts and Precious Works: *Archief Paul Fredericq* [hereinafter abbreviated to: *Archief Fredericq*], Hs. 3704/I.
> *Archief Fredericq*, 2991/I: memorandum 10 November 1905.

The documents in the archive mentioned above are not ordered by inventory number but by manuscript number. In practice, it boils down to the same thing. Please note that **Ms.** (in Dutch: **Hs**) stands for manuscript.

In general, the details of a document's location should be rendered in a sequence from general to detailed information. A possible exception to this rule is when the title or nature of the document and the date of entry is mentioned first.

> Instruction for Aremberg 6-12-1553, Algemeen Rijksarchief Brussels, Papiers d'État et de l'Audience, inv.no. 784, f. 213.

Many institutions that hold archives have citation instructions for authors who wish to refer to documents from the institution's collections. Such instructions are usually found in the archive's inventory. For instance, if you look at the catalogue of the University Library in Leiden, you will find:

> Researchers who wish to refer to this collection should report the following information: University Library Leiden, Curators' Archive, 1574-1815. Please refer to the individual documents as follows: ACI [inventory number].

One of the documents is designated as follows in the catalogue:

> 17. Contents: Rough notes, taken by the Secretary J. de Fremery. Dated: 1807-1811. Form: 1 cover.

A reference to this item in a footnote or endnote would look like this:

> University Library Leiden, Curators' Archive, 1574-1815, AC1 inv. no. 17, Rough notes, taken by the Secretary J. de Fremery, 1807-1811.

I.1.6   Referring to a newspaper article

A reference to a newspaper article consists of the headline above the relevant article, the name of the newspaper, and the date on which it was published. It can be compared to a reference from a scientific journal; the article's title should be placed between quotation marks, and the name of the paper should be printed in italics. The date should also be given between brackets.

> 'Tweede Kamer', *Tilburgsche Courant* (26 February 1905).

If the author's name is known, you should include it at the beginning of the reference.

> Taft Kiser, 'Open Season on History', *The New York Times* (2 August 2013).

More or less the same rules apply to references to other non-academic periodicals such as magazines. As well as the aforementioned information, you should also include the number of the relevant volume after the name of the medium.

I.1.7   Referring to an unpublished article or paper

If you need to refer to unpublished texts, record the title of the writing in straight (Roman) letters, without quotation marks. A description of the nature of the text and its year of origin between brackets should follow the author and the title.

> J.M. Kamp, With the assistance of armed men. The cross-community migration of Swiss soldiers in the United Provinces, 1750-1850 (Research Master's thesis for History, Vrije Universiteit, Amsterdam 2012).

I.1.8   Notes to visual sources

The sequence may vary according to the reasons for including an image. However, the following elements should be included for the most complete caption possible of images (photographs, paintings, prints, recordings of an item, etc.):

> Title (or brief description); maker; location; dates; material; size; the location where it can be found or is held.

This information should be added as a caption to the image in the text or put in a list of illustrations at the back, along with the archives and the literature you have used, with a brief caption in the body text.

For example: if you were to use a famous picture by Jan Toorop for a discussion in a cultural-historical context, you would write a brief caption:

> Jan Toorop, *The Three Brides*, 1892-1893.

In the list of illustrations, you could write:

> Jan Toorop, *The Three Brides*, 1892-1893. Pencil, Conté, coloured chalk, white highlights, crayon and pencil on brown cardboard. 78 x 98 cm. Collection of the Kröller-Müller Museum, Otterlo, inv.no. 800-19.

You could also put your 'own' caption to an image in the body text, as long as you add all the details about the image (in the caption or in the list of illustrations). For instance, a caption added to a drawing of the Waterfront in Paramaribo, seen from the river, could state, in the body text:

> This tent boat with eight oarsmen seems to be on its way to Fort Zeelandia, 1797.

However, you must also include a full description:

> *View of Paramaribo*, anonymous (ca. 1800). Oil on canvas. 67.8 x 114.6 cm. Collection of the National Maritime Museum in Amsterdam (A. 3535).

Remember that these rules apply to photographs, too. Photographs may be printed and reproduced more often; unlike unique paintings, it can be difficult to find the most 'original' version and place where it is held. In that case, give the source where you found the photograph. For example:

> 9 September 1943, refugees and Italian soldiers on Col de Cerise. Collection of M. Raiberti, reproduced in *De Groene Amsterdammer* 16-4-2015, p. 30.

I.1.9 Notes to databases, tables, and figures

Even if you are referring to a database, you must apply the annotation rules as accurately as possible. You must at least state the maker(s), the title (or a description of the subject), the location where it can be found or is held, and a long-term link to databases that are available online. For example:

> A.H. Bollemeijer, 'Demography of Batavia, 1689-1789', EASY DANS, https://easy.dans.knaw.nl, persistent identifier: urn:nbn:nl:ui:13-yohp-dg (1989/2010).

You must always provide the correct titles and indications of the units if you are referring to a chart or a table (in the table or along the axes of the chart). Give a number to figures and tables if you use more than one. Always mention the source(s) from which you obtained the data under the figures or tables. The sources might be from an archive, from other people's databases, or from information reported in publications by other authors, as illustrated by the following figure, taken from Matthias van Rossum, 'De Intra-Aziatische vaart. Schepen, "de Aziatische zeeman" en ondergang van de voc?', *Tijdschrift voor Sociale en Economische Geschiedenis* 8:3 (2011) 32-69, q.v. 40:

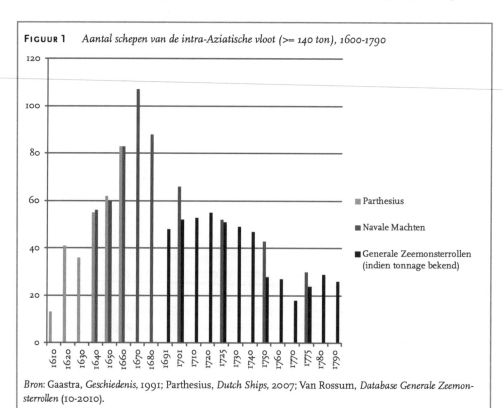

FIGUUR 1   *Aantal schepen van de intra-Aziatische vloot (>= 140 ton), 1600-1790*

■ Parthesius

■ Navale Machten

■ Generale Zeemonsterrollen (indien tonnage bekend)

Bron: Gaastra, *Geschiedenis*, 1991; Parthesius, *Dutch Ships*, 2007; Van Rossum, *Database Generale Zeemonsterrollen* (10-2010).

I.1.10   Consecutive notes

Historical works use footnotes or endnotes to make references. The rules for annotation are the same for both types of notes. If two consecutive notes refer to the same work, you can put 'Ibidem' under the second note instead of the author and title. Ibidem is Latin for 'at the same place'. If two consecutive notes refer to a different page of the same work, use 'Ibidem' followed by a comma and the page number.

Below is an example of a list with six footnotes or endnotes to a fictional text. The second note refers to the same page as the first note. The third note refers to the same work but to a different page. Because a reference is made to another work in the fourth note, the fifth note should include the title again. The sixth note refers to the same work as the fifth note but to a different page.

> 1) J. Huizinga, *Herfsttij der Middeleeuwen. Studie over levens- en gedachtenvormen der veertiende en vijftiende eeuw in Frankrijk en de Nederlanden* (seventh edition; Haarlem 1950) 93.
> 2) Ibidem.
> 3) Ibidem, 106.
> 4) Jacob Burckhardt, *Die Kultur der Renaissance in Italien* (Frankfurt am Main 1989).
> 5) Huizinga, *Herfsttij der Middeleeuwen*, 100.
> 6) Ibidem, 102.

You are not *obliged* to use 'Ibidem' and using it poses the risk that, if parts of the text are moved around in the final edit, you could lose the title to which the note refers. 'Ibidem' is also not very practical if you are using EndNote. Sometimes, it could be easier simply to use shortened titles instead of 'Ibidem'.

I.1.11   Grouped notes

It is possible to refer to more than one title in a note if information from the annotated passage relies on information from several works. The same rules apply here as with notes in which only one title is referred to: if the title is rendered for the first time, it should be given in full, while shorter rendering will suffice if the title has already been mentioned in a previous note. However, if one of the titles in a grouped note is the same as in the previous note, the relevant title is best rendered in a shorter version again. The use of 'Ibidem' in a grouped note is not permitted. The different titles in a grouped note should be separated from each other by a semi-colon. A full stop only follows after the last title, thus:

> A. Th. van Deursen, *Een hoeksteen in een verzuild bestel. De Vrije Universiteit 1880-2005* (Amsterdam 2005) 107; A. Th. van Deursen, 'De Vrije Universiteit en de geschiedwetenschappen' in: *Wetenschap en rekenschap 1880-1980* (Kampen 1980) 360.

I.1.12   Abbreviations in notes

Sometimes, certain terms or abbreviations are used in footnotes or endnotes to indicate whether the title that follows should be viewed in a certain light in connection to the annotated passage. **Cf.** (in Dutch: **Vgl.**) stands for 'confer'. The author is referring to a work in which something else is claimed than what is said in the annotated passage. The reader is invited to consider various points of view. If the author refers to a viewpoint that explicitly contrasts with the argument he or she is putting forward in the annotated passage, but that polemic is not given in the passage, the author can use the term **Other** (in Dutch: **Anders:**). De abbreviation **e.g.** (in Dutch: **Bijv.**) means 'for example'. In such cases, the author is referring to one or more works that contain examples of what is said in the annotated passage. The claims in the annotated passage do not, therefore, rely only on the title in the note. The title to which the author refers can be exchanged for others. In this case, the terms **Among others** (in Dutch: **Onder meer**) and **See** (in Dutch: **Zie**) are sometimes used. These terms and abbreviations are also given before the reference to the work. Thus:

> Cf. Sarah van Walsum, *The family and the nation. Dutch family migration policies in the context of changing family norms* (Newcastle upon Tyne 2008).

I.2   The bibliography

A bibliography or list of sources should be provided at the end of a book, article, thesis, or assignment. In fact, most journal articles will also end with a bibliography. The bibliography should include all the titles used for the work, even if no reference is made to those works in the footnotes or endnotes. The only exception to this rule are general historical reference works that are only used to verify a few facts: these do not need to be included in the bibliography.

I.2.1   Rules of thumb for a bibliography

1. Make a distinction between primary and secondary sources. All the books, collections, and articles – printed or available in digital format – you have used should be included in the same list. Separate entries should be made for items from archives, other non-printed sources (including websites as primary sources), and non-academic publications such as newspaper articles and interviews. This also applies to museum collections you have consulted and image archives. A separate list should be made for each archive and newspaper from which several items have been used in which they are all listed.

2. The order of titles. The reference list should be given in alphabetical order according to the (first) author's surname. If several works by the same author have been used, they should be listed in reversed chronological order: the most recent title should be at the top. Publications from the same year should be given an a, b, c, etc. following the year (e.g. 1998a, 1998b, etc.). All titles should be rendered in the same way as in the footnotes or endnotes. The only exception to this is that the first name or initial(s) of the first author listed should be placed behind his or her family name (surname), so that the alphabetical order is clear. If a title covers several lines, the second and following lines should be indented so that it is clear when the list provides the next title.

3. Mentioning of page numbers. The bibliography should not provide page numbers for books listed in it, even if only part of that book was read for the paper in question. Nonetheless, when listing articles in collections and articles in journals, you should provide the page numbers of the relevant articles in the collection or journal.

4. Shared authorship. If the title page does not include any name of an author, for example, if the work is one to which a number of writers have contributed, the title should be categorised according to the first letter of the title, not including definite or indefinite articles.

5. Each reference item should be concluded with a full stop.

> Bentley, M., *Modern historiography. An introduction* (London-New York 2003).
>
> Bentley, M., 'The evolution and dissemination of historical knowledge' in: M. Danton ed., *The organization of knowledge in Victorian Britain* (Oxford 2005) 173-197.
>
> Berger, S., M. Donovan and K. Passmore ed., *Writing national histories. Western Europe since 1800* (London-New York 1999).

I.3 Summarizing diagram

Diagram 5: Overview of cited examples of annotation according to 'De Buck Style'.

Reference to:	
Book in a footnote, full title description (first edition)	J. Huizinga, *Herfsttij der Middeleeuwen. Studie over levens- en gedachtenvormen der veertiende en vijftiende eeuw in Frankrijk en de Nederlanden* (Haarlem 1919).
Book in a footnote, full title description (later edition)	J. Huizinga, *Herfsttij der Middeleeuwen. Studie over levens- en gedachtenvormen der veertiende en vijftiende eeuw in Frankrijk en de Nederlanden* (33rd edition; Amsterdam 2012).
Book in a footnote, abbreviated description (with reference to pages)	Huizinga, *Herfsttij der Middeleeuwen*, 66-75, 106.
Book with translator in a footnote, full title description	Karl R. Popper, *De armoede van het historicisme*, transl. G. van den Bergh (Amsterdam 1967).
Book as part of a series in a footnote, full title description	Frank McDonough, *The Origins of the First and Second World Wars*. Cambridge Perspectives in History (Cambridge 1997).
Published source with editor in a footnote, full title description	Samuel Pepys, *The illustrated Pepys: extracts from the diary*. Robert Latham ed. (London 1978).
Article in a journal in a footnote, full title description (with reference to pages)	Elizabeth Edwards, 'Photographic uncertainties: evidence and reassurance', *History and Anthropology* 25:2 (2014) 171-188, q.v. 178.
Article in a journal in a footnote, abbreviated title description (with reference to pages)	Edwards, 'Photographic uncertainties', 178.
Article in a collection footnote, full title description (with reference to pages)	J.C. Kennedy, 'Religion, Nation and European Representations of the of the Past' in: Stefan Berger and Chris Lorenz eds., *The Contested Nation: Ethnicity, Class, Religion and Class, Religion and Gender in National Histories* (Basingstoke 2008) 104-134, q.v. 108-109.

Diagram 5 (continued): Overview of cited examples of annotation according to 'De Buck Style'.

Reference to:	
Article in a collection in a footnote, abbreviated title description (with reference to pages)	Kennedy, 'Religion, Nation', 108-109.
Article in a collection of work by the same author in a footnote, full title description	Geoffrey Roberts, 'J.H. Hexter: Narrative History and Common Sense' in Idem, *The History and Narrative Reader* (London and New York 2001) 135-139
Collection without an editor on the title page, full title description	*Wetenschap en rekenschap, 1880-1980. Een eeuw wetenschapsbeoefening en wetenschapsbeschouwing aan de Vrije Universiteit* (Kampen 1980)
Publication included in a collected work in a footnote, full title description	Robert Fruin, 'Over het bewaren van het lijk voor het proces bij de Friezen' (1886) in: Idem, *Verspreide Geschriften* VIII (The Hague 1903) 147-148.
Website, full title description	Internet Encyclopedia of Philosophy, www.iep.utm.edu (consulted 15 August 2014).
Article in a journal in a footnote, full title description including DOI	Karel Davids, 'River Control and the Evolution of Knowledge: A Comparison Between Regions in China and Europe, c. 1400-1850', *Journal of Global History* 1:1 (March 2006): 59-79. DOI: 10.1017/S1740022806000040.
Archive item	University Library Leiden, Archive K.H. Roessingh (BPL 2825), inv.no. 22, lecture 'Troeltsch' (1915).
Newspaper article without author, full title description	'Tweede Kamer', *Tilburgsche Courant* (26 February 1905).
Newspaper article with author in a footnote, full title description	Taft Kiser, 'Open Season on History', *The New York Times* (2 August 2013).
Unpublished thesis in a footnote, full title description	J.M. Kamp, With the assistance of armed men. The cross-community migration of Swiss soldiers in the United Provinces, 1750-1850 (Research Master's thesis for History, Vrije Universiteit, Amsterdam 2012).

Diagram 5 (continued): Overview of cited examples of annotation according to 'De Buck Style'.

Reference to:	
A number of title references in a footnote	A. Th. van Deursen, *Een hoeksteen in een verzuild bestel. De Vrije Universiteit 1880-2005* (Amsterdam 2005) 107; A. Th. van Deursen, 'De Vrije Universiteit en de geschiedwetenschappen' in: *Wetenschap en rekenschap 1880-1980* (Kampen 1980) 360.
Bibliography	Bentley, M., *Modern historiography. Introduction* (London-New York 2003). Bentley, M., 'The evolution and dissemination of historical knowledge' in: M. Daunton ed., *The organization of knowledge in Victorian Britain* (Oxford 2005) 173-197. Berger, S., M. Donovan, and K. Passmore eds., *Writing national histories: Western Europe since 1800* (London-New York 1999).

Notes

1   De Buck, *Zoeken en schrijven.*

2   Taken from Jan Guichelaar, George B. Huitema, and Hylkje de Jong eds., *Zekerheden in waarheden. Natuurwetenschappelijke ontwikkelingen in Nederland rond 1900* (Hilversum 2012); F.H. Sysling, *The archipelago of difference. Physical anthropology in the Netherlands Indies, ca. 1890-1960* (Amsterdam 2013).

Appendix II
Other styles of notes

The 'De Buck Style' of annotation described in Appendix I is the most relevant style in the Netherlands. It is also commonly used abroad and is available in EndNote. It is often prescribed by Dutch universities and universities of applied sciences and frequently used as a basis for author's' guidelines for historical publishers and journal editors. However, other annotation styles are used in the Netherlands as well.

II.1   Variations on 'De Buck'

Some Dutch authors choose to use a style that differs somewhat from 'De Buck' in certain ways. We are talking about small matters, such as a comma in front of 'in', leaving out the brackets around the place and date of an edition, or the use of 'p.' or 'pp.' to indicate page numbers when rendering numbers.

> E.H. Carr, *What is history?*, London 1975.
> 'Hermeneutiek en deconstructie', in: Th. de Boer e.a., *Hermeneutiek. Filosofische grondslagen van mens en cultuurwetenschappen*, Meppel/Amsterdam 1988, p. 218.

Authors may also name the publisher of the work as well as the place of publication. The reference below also mentions the year of the original edition (between brackets) as well as the year of the edition or version the author consulted. The number 28 refers to a page number.

> Ernest Renan, *Qu'est-ce qu'une nation?* Leiden: Academic Press Leiden (1882) 1994, 28.

In your course, you will be trained to annotate very accurately and systematically with the 'De Buck Style'. Even if you decide to deviate from this style later, there are two principles you should bear in mind:

1. Use your style of annotation consistently. Make sure that you are very familiar with it so that you do not waste time putting your notes in the right order. Some programmes such as EndNote can help you keep track.
2. Do not create a style of your own but follow a style that is used by others in the same field. Save your creativeness for the text itself. The purpose of references is to help the reader find the cited passages with ease. This means that it must be possible for the reader to see the information on which you have based your text at a glance.

That does not mean that a reference should never include information that does not suit an existing style of annotation. Extra information that is relevant to finding the source to which you refer may (or must) always be provided. Always remember that the references are intended to help the reader trace the source you cite as easily as possible.

II.2   The Chicago Style

As we have seen above, styles of annotation vary per country. In English-language publications, a whole range of different styles are used. Historians primarily use the Chicago Style, which is named after *The Chicago Manual of Style* published by the University of Chicago Press.[1] Dutch historians are increasingly becoming involved in English-language academic circles, and Dutch university curriculums often include more English publications than Dutch ones. We would therefore recommend that you become familiar with the Chicago Style too. The differences between the annotation style we introduced above and the Chicago Style are not huge, but pay attention to the punctuation in the examples explained below.

When you refer to a book, the words in the title are capitalised, with the exception of definite and indefinite articles, prepositions, and conjunctions. The publisher is also mentioned, following the place of publication and separated from it by a colon.

> Jane Burbank and Frederick Cooper, *Empires in World History: Power and the Politics of Difference* (Princeton and Oxford: Princeton University Press, 2010), 23.

And the shorter version, with page numbers:

> Burbank and Cooper, *Empires*, 23.

If translated, the translator is placed between the title and place of publication, preceded by the abbreviation **trans**. In the bibliography, 'Translated by' should not be abbreviated, and a full stop should follow the title.

> Leo Tolstoy, *War and Peace: A Novel*, trans. Louise and Aylmer Maude (Glasgow: The University Press, 1938).

In the bibliography:

> Leo Tolstoy, *War and Peace: A Novel*. Translated by Louise and Aylmer Maude. Glasgow: The University Press, 1938.

If you refer to a few specific pages in an article, use the word 'at', followed by the page numbers.

> W. Windelband, "History and Natural Science," trans. G. Oakes, *History and Theory* 19 (1980): 169-85, at 175, 177, 179.

You can leave them out in the bibliography:

> Windelband, W. "History and Natural Science." Translated by G. Oakes.
> *History and Theory* 19 (1980): 169-85.

Sometimes when a reference is made to an article in a journal, the number of the relevant issue as well as the number of the volume is given. It should follow the number of the volume, separated by a comma and preceded by the abbreviation **no.** (number). In some references, the number of the year of publication is rendered as an abbreviation **vol.** (for volume). Its use depends on the publisher's style rules.

> Christof Dejung, "'Switzerland must be a special democracy': Sociopolitical Compromise, Military Comradeship, and the Gender Order in 1930s and 1940s Switzerland," *Journal of Modern History* 82, no. 1 (March 2010): 101-126.

> Fearghal McGarry, "Twentieth-century Ireland Revisited," *Journal of Contemporary History* vol. 42, no. 1 (January 2007): 117-136.

In the notes system for English-language texts, 'Ibidem' is usually abbreviated to **Ibid.**

In the bibliography, titles are rendered slightly differently than in the footnotes or endnotes. For books, brackets are not used (though they are used for articles in journals; see above for an example), and the use of punctuation varies a little too.

> Anderson, Fred, and Andrew R.L. Cayton. *The Dominion of War: Empire and Liberty in North America, 1500-2000.* New York: Viking, 2005.
> Armitage, David, ed. *Theories of Empire, 1450-1800.* Brookfield: Ashgate, 1998.
> Hamilton, Carolyn, *Terrific Majesty: The Powers of Shaka Zulu and the Limits of Historical Invention.* Cambridge, MA and London: Harvard University Press, 1998.

The *Chicago Manual of Style* also gives instructions for a reference to a review, which should first give the name of the reviewer, followed by the title of the review. That is followed first by the title of the reviewed work, preceded by the words 'review of'. Next comes the author of that work, preceded by 'by' and, finally, the medium is given in which the review can be found. The details of the specific number of the medium and the page numbers are rendered in the same way as in the references to an article in a journal:

Robert Finlay, "How Not to (Re)Write World History: Gavin Menzies and the Chinese Discovery of America," review of *1421: The Year China Discovered the World*, by Gavin Menzies, *Journal of World History* 15, no. 2 (June 2004): 229-242.

And the shorter version:

Finlay, "How Not to (Re)Write World History."

The bibliography should list the review alphabetically according to the reviewer's surname. An anonymous review is alphabetised according to the name of the medium in which it was published.

Diagram 6: Overview of cited examples of annotation according to the Chicago Style

Reference to:	
Book in a footnote, abbreviated title description (with reference to pages)	Burbank and Cooper, *Empires*, 23.
Book in the bibliography, full title description	Jane Burbank and Frederick Cooper, *Empires in World History: History: Power and the Politics of Difference* (Princeton and Oxford: Princeton University Press, 2010), 23.
Book with translator in a footnote, full title description	Leo Tolstoy, *War and Peace: A Novel*, trans. Louise and Aylmer Maude (Glasgow: The University Press, 1938).
Book with translator in a bibliography, full title description	Leo Tolstoy, *War and Peace: A Novel*. Translated by Louise and Aylmer Maude Glasgow: The University Press, 1938.
Article in a journal in a footnote, full title description	W. Windelband, "History and Natural Science," trans. G. Oakes, *History and Theory* 19 (1980): 169-85, at 175, 177, 179.
Article in a journal in a bibliography, full title description	Windelband, W. "History and Natural Science." Translated by G. Oakes. *History and Theory* 19 (1980): 169-85.
Article in a journal in a footnote with volume and issue, full title description	Fearghal McGarry, "Twentieth-century Ireland Revisited," *Journal of Contemporary History* vol. 42, no. 1 (January 2007): 117-136.

Diagram 6 (continued): Overview of cited examples of annotation according to the Chicago Style

Reference to:	
Review in a footnote, full title description	Robert Finlay, "How Not to (Re)Write World History: Gavin Menzies and the Chinese Discovery of America," review of 1421: *The Year China Discovered the World*, by Gavin Menzies. *Journal of World History* 15, no. 2 (June 2004): 229-242.
Review in a footnote, abbreviated title description	Finlay, "How Not to (Re)Write World History."
Review in the bibliography: full title description	Finlay, Robert, "How Not to (Re)Write World History: Gavin Menzies and the Chinese Discovery of America," review of 1421: *The Year China Discovered the World*, by Gavin Menzies, *Journal of World History* 15, no. 2 (June 2004): 229-242.

II. 3   Author-date references

In addition to the version we have discussed above, there is a second version of the Chicago Style used for reference. That system is called *author-date reference*. It is a system that is particularly common in the field of natural sciences but is used very frequently in the social sciences too. In historical publications, this method of annotation is almost never used, but because more and more interdisciplinary research is being done, historians are using literatures in which this style of annotation is used more and more often. Moreover, historians regularly publish in social-scientific journals that use this system. For author-date references, notes are not used to refer to other titles; rather, the reference is included in the body text. In such cases, notes only serve to digress briefly from the main subject, to give a short explanation or to otherwise elaborate briefly. The reference to the cited literature in the text is rendered by placing the author's surname and the year of publication between brackets after the passage in the text to which the reference pertains. The reader can then check, in a reference list at the back of the book (or sometimes after each chapter), which title this reference applies to.

We have used a passage from *De constructie van het verleden* by Chris Lorenz as an example of this. The first example uses the system with footnotes or endnotes while the second example has an author-date reference.

> In the last decade, under the influence of post-modernism in history, scep-tical doubts have once again been expressed about the possibility to acquire reliable knowledge about the past. For instance, American historian William McNeill suggested to regard all historiography as *mythistory* ('mythical history') because all historical knowledge is uncertain.[1]

That means that the footnotes or endnotes should say:

> [1] W. McNeill, *Mythistory and Other Essays* (Chicago: University of Chicago Press, 1986) 1-43.

If Lorenz were to have used the author-date reference system, the reference would have looked like this:

> In the last decade, under the influence of post-modernism in history, scep-tical doubts have once again been expressed about the possibility to acquire reliable knowledge about the past. For instance, American historian William McNeill suggested to regard all historiography as *mythistory* ('mythical history') because all historical knowledge is uncertain (McNeill 1986, 1-43).

Only the *List of references* at the back of the book contains the full title:

> McNeill, W. 1986. *Mythistory and Other Essays*. Chicago: University of Chicago Press.

That list of references, which should correspond to the references in the text, is arranged alphabetically according to the surnames of the (first) authors. Accordingly, the (first) author's first name or initials after the surnames should be included in a bibliography in a work that uses foot-notes or endnotes.

One deviation from a bibliography in a work that only uses footnotes or endnotes is that the *List of references* in a work using author-date reference gives the year of publication immediately following the author's name. For instance, the reference in the text can be linked in one glance to the correct title in the list of references. In addition, titles by the same author are not ar-ranged alphabetically according to their titles as is the case in a bibliography but listed chronologically according to their year of publication. Any page numbers are not included in the list of references but given in the reference in the text. In the example above, there is a reference to pages 1 to 43.

If the author's name is also mentioned in the passage, it is sometimes left out from the reference. The text above already mentions that the idea discussed was suggested by William McNeill and the reference could, in that case, also look like this:

(1986, 1-43).

As this reference follows a sentence in which McNeill is mentioned, it is clear that the year 1986 pertains to a work by this historian. If an author has published two different works in the same year, they are distinguished in the reference by adding a small case 'a' or 'b' behind the year. In the list of references, those letters are obviously placed after the year so that the references in the text can be linked to the right titles.

In a text that discusses the work of Groningen historical philosopher Frank Ankersmit, you might see the following two references, for example:

(Ankersmit 1996a)
(Ankersmit 1996b)

The list of references would, in this case, state:

Ankersmit, F.R. 1996a. *De Spiegel van het Verleden. Exploraties deel I: Geschiedtheorie.* Kampen: Kok Agora.
Ankersmit, F.R. 1996b. *De Macht van Representatie. Exploraties deel II: Cultuurfilosofie en Esthetica.* Kampen: Kok Agora.

A reference to a title by two authors should include both names. In references to works by more than two authors, generally speaking, only the name of the first author is given, followed by the abbreviation used in English-language publications **et al.** (*et alii*, which means 'and others'). In Dutch-language texts, the abbreviation **e.a.** might be used. A reference to a work by two authors (whether they are the compilers of the work or not) should be given as follows in the text:

(Clancy-Smith and Gouda 1998)

Additional details, such as when you are referring to the editors of a collection, are absent from the reference in the text. The reader cannot deduce from the references whether the reference concerns a book, a collection, or an article in a journal. To find out, he or she must look at the list of references. For instance, the list of references would, in the case of the reference above, include:

Clancy-Smith, Julia and Frances Gouda eds. 1998. *Domesticating the Empire: Race, Gender, and Family Life in French and Dutch Colonialism.* Charlottesville and London: University Press of Virginia.

It is possible that a reference needs to include several author-date references. In such cases, the title references are separated by a semicolon. Such references may also include page numbers. The titles can be arranged either chronologically (year of publication) or alphabetically (by surname).

An example of this type of reference might look like this:

(Ankersmit 1996; McNeill 1986)

If a single reference pertains to several titles by the same author, the author's name is not repeated; it is sufficient – after the first full reference – to give the years. Such references look like this:

(Ankersmit 1996a, 1996b)

Very occasionally, a book will combine the use of footnotes with author-date references. In such cases, the text has footnotes, but they only state the author's name and the year of publication. The reader can check the list of references to see to which title it refers. This system of author-date references is not popular among historians because they do not use footnotes or endnotes to refer to titles but also for providing background information without interrupting the flow of the author's argument. The combination of author-date references and footnotes is somewhat forced, especially if more references need to be made in the notes. Author-date references are not suitable for references to primary sources either.

The 15th and 16th editions of *The Chicago Manuel of Style* are available online at www.chicagomanualofstyle.org. If you want to access the entire contents, you will need to subscribe, but it is possible to get a free trial subscription for 30 days.

Note

1   The Chicago Manual of Style. University of Chicago Press, 2010 (16th edition) is also available as an online *resource*: www.chicagomanualofstyle.org/home. html.

Acknowledgements

Geschiedenis schrijven! (Writing History!) is the joint effort of four authors. Our motive was a need to write a new 'De Buck', the usual 'guide in the Netherlands to writing a historical paper' written by a group of authors: Piet de Buck, Carla Musterd, Nicolette Moud, and Jaap Talsma. Generations of historians, including the authors of this guide, were trained using 'De Buck'.[1] Piet de Buck, an early-modern historian, and his fellow authors, lecturer Carla Musterd and Nicolette Mout, now emeritus professor of Modern History, worked in Leiden. Jaap Talsma was a historian of the late-modern and contemporary period at the History Department of the University of Amsterdam. Many elements of their guide still have unimpaired relevance, and for this new guide we stick to the 'De Buck' standards for annotation rules for historical publications without any alterations. Nonetheless, times and technology have changed so much that many aspects of the historian's craft require a new manual.

The authors collective that compiled *Writing History!* was formed in 2013 at the Vrije Universiteit Amsterdam. Sebas Rümke completed the Research Master in Global History and has taken up a doctoral candidate (PhD) position at the *Doktorandenkolleg China in Europe, Europe in China* of the University of Hamburg. After receiving the Research Master degree in Early Modern History at the vu, Jeannette Kamp moved to Leiden University, where she completed her doctorate on the history of crime and gender in early modern Frankfurt. Matthias van Rossum, who received his doctorate at the vu Amsterdam in 2013, worked as lecturer at Leiden University and is now Senior Researcher at the International Institute for Social History in Amsterdam. Susan Legêne is Professor of Political History at vu Amsterdam. Prior to that position, she worked at the Royal Tropical Institute /Tropenmuseum and was endowed professor at the University of Amsterdam, where she graduated in 1982. The members of the group complement each other well both in terms of age and study background in relation to their fields and their knowledge of various history programmes.

During the 2014/2015 academic year, the manuscript of *Writing History!* was used for teaching the first-year course Academic Skills (ACVA) and the second-year introductory courses for the History programme at VU Amsterdam. We are grateful to our fellow lecturers and our students for their suggestions for improving it. Above all, we owe thanks to Jaap Talsma, who painstakingly checked the Dutch edition of the manuscript in his characteristic way. His notes are the bridge between 'De Buck' and this new companion, and we are extremely grateful for his dedication. Many thanks to Jacco Pekelder, too, the reviewer for Amsterdam University Press who carefully inspected the manuscript. We also owe much to Rem ter Hofstede, the history specialist at the VU Library (Universiteitsbibliotheek VU Amsterdam, or UBVU), and are grateful for his notes on the description of the search and discovery of historical-academic literature. Libraries are evolving extremely quickly and are a hugely important aspect of the changing context of historiography. *Writing History!* assumes the current state of affairs and attempts to offer prospective historians a foundation on which to deal with the developments in ICT. It is exciting to actively watch how our field is developing. We hope that this book will accompany prospective historians to become active players in these developments.

Note

1   De Buck, *Zoeken en schrijven.*

INDEX